Life Behind the Staffroom Door

Jackson Barker

Life Behind the Staffroom Door by Jackson Barker
Copyright © 2022. All rights reserved.

Published by Pen It! Publications, LLC in the U.S.A.
812-371-4128
www.penitpublications.com

ISBN: 978-1-63984-218-6
Cover Design by Donna Cook
Editing by Leah Pugh

Dedicated to you, F.L.

Acknowledgements

Thanks to Little Hare for being patient, proof reading, listening to my moronic and non-stop rambling, and always driving the belief that I could do this. I shared the worst of my teaching experiences with you, and you made them better. Mum and Dad, as well as 'other mum,' you listened to the ideas, never once discouraged me, and also shared my vision. The schools I've worked in for the experiences I've had, which have helped shape this book. The children I have taught, for all your many, many questions, strange little ways, and shared experiences. My best friend and beautiful dog, Jack, for all the love, cuddles, companionship, and never wavering tail wags whilst I battled through this project. As well as the constant reminder that at the end of every chapter, there would always be a walk needed. For the many more people and experiences we shared throughout my teaching career, thank you to you all

Table of Contents

Introduction

What do teachers talk about behind the staffroom door? What do teachers really think about the children they teach? Is the life of a teacher as cushy as starting work at 8 a.m. and leaving at 4 p.m.? What drives and motivates a teacher? Is your child's teacher really the pillar of the community, they appear to be?

At the age of twenty-five I decided to give up a full-time job in the financial sector and go to university for three years to train as a primary school teacher. Much to the amusement of everyone who knew me. I survived the ECT[1] year with all it threw at me and taught until I was forty-two. Countless school trips, parents' evenings, after school clubs lesson observations eventually broke my spirit and I left the profession. A system full of bureaucracy, hypocrisy, and make believe had drained all the aspiration and fun out of me and made me question my career choice.

---

[1] Early Career Teachers

From my experience, I found out what teaching is actually like, what makes a good teacher, and eventually found out what goes on behind the staffroom door. This book will lift the lid on the good, the bad, and the ugly behind your local primary school gates.

In this book you'll read about the highs and lows of being a primary school teacher. You'll hear about the reality behind the theory and understand some of the antics which occur after you've dropped your child off at the school gate.

The Interview Process

Teaching, where every lesson shapes a life
Searching for the 'ideal school'

Regardless of the job, interviews are daunting. Once you find out you've been successful, you have a period of time known as the build-up to research the prospective company, try and find out as much as you can about them, and keep a few essential nuggets of information in mind about them. So, if asked or questioned, you can fire out this information with relative ease in a conversation. After research, you spend time deciding what to wear, how to smell, and how you can come across as the best candidate ever seen.

Prior to the interview stage, there is far more to do than just decide 'this is the school for me'.

Firstly, you need to research the school doing the advertising. What did their last Ofsted look like? What is attendance and behaviour like? Is this a transient school? What is staff retention like?

Location to where I live or travel time? All of these questions need addressing before step two, the school visit.

The School Visit

You've decided it's a school you'd like to work in, so you need to arrange a visit. Now, if you are currently working in a school, looking for time off to visit another school is a tricky issue. How will you approach it without arousing suspicion that you're thinking of leaving? I would suggest a doctor's appointment, or a day off sick. It worked for me, and I was never questioned. Not very moral, but better than the shit storm caused by announcing you're thinking about leaving! If this is your first school visit / interview, this won't be an issue.

A school visit prior to applying is always a great idea. You will get a sense as soon as you walk in what type of school it is. Usually the waiting area / reception and the displays give an idea. Schools love to show off awards. If the school you are visiting has any, they will be proudly displayed in the reception / waiting area. This always made me laugh, looking at the school 'wall of pride'.

These were usually awards/achievements ranging from: 'Ofsted rated outstanding' to such boasts as '£123.43 raised for Comic Relief'. What always made me laugh was seeing the dates these awards were presented. 'Ofsted rated outstanding 2013', yet you're awaiting a school tour today, 2019. 'Greenest school 2011', 'fittest school 2012'. Ironically, I read this as a reasonably tubby child shuffled their way past me, out of the door, and to the nearest ice-cream van no doubt.

While I appreciate the need for schools to display their pride in their achievements, is it really relevant to any visitor that the school took part in a spelling-bee five years ago and raised £35.00 for the local cat's home?

At some point several other interested parties will join you. Here is your first opportunity to size up the competition. While everyone who arrives will give an awkward, friendly smile, each one of these people are vying for the job you want. Each one of them will have done the research you did and will try to be noticed during the upcoming tour of the school.

Eventually, a member of staff will greet you and welcome you to the school. This may be the head, could be an <u>SLT</u> member, or whoever else was free that evening. You'll be given a welcome speech, which usually involves a history of the school, how well they are doing, and how happy their staff are. At some point you and the other visitors will be broken into two groups, depending on the number of prospective applicants.

From there, you'll be shown around the school as if you were taking part in a guided museum tour. The best prepared classrooms will be viewed. This is where you may see the odd teacher still slumped over their workstation, or an after-school club just wrapping up for the evening.

You'll be talked through the various displays mounted in classrooms, halls, and adjoining corridors. You'll be swept through ICT suites, staffrooms, and carefully prepared intervention areas. All-in-all the school tour is nothing short of a parade to show off examples of well prepared, neat and tidy classrooms, pristine displays, and the odd 'perky, over smiley' member of staff who may still be visible during the evening.

Next, you'll all be gathered together and, in some cases, told about the role which is being advertised. You will be told the role has come about due to one of three things: Staff development, pupil growth, or proposed expansion to the school. This is where you need to listen. Why does the school need another teacher? Has someone left, if so, why? Are more pupils joining the school and as a result the school is expanding? Is it that the school has enrolled more children for next year, but are not expanding? In other words, larger class sizes.

You will be offered the opportunity to ask any questions. This is where you may decide you want to stand out. Do you ask about the results of the last Ofsted? Is it wise to ask about pupil progress? Do you want to find out what year group the vacancy is for? This is where people are hoping to be remembered by the member of staff who is carrying out the tour. It's always interesting to see who raises a question, how it's received, and what the response is.

Finally, you'll be escorted out and reminded to sign out of the visitor's book. My recommendation here is to try to be the last to sign out. Why? This is your opportunity to scan the visitor's names and look under the 'visiting from' column to see who is currently employed in a school and who is not. Where are these perspective applicants coming from? If they are already employed, what school are they coming from? Is it a school that may also be advertising once this person informs them they are looking elsewhere? All of this is useful information.

So, you've done the groundwork, visited the school, got a feel for the place, maybe even grabbed a word with a member of staff on the way out. Next comes the application form.

The Application Form

L ike all jobs, the application form is standard. List your personal details, hobbies, interests, and work experience. If you're an <u>ECT,</u> this will be all the places you worked pre-university and during your degree. Unlike other application forms, you are asked to briefly list all the reasons you are the right person for the job.

Here you have to mention: your school visit and what your impressions were, why you feel (Based on that visit) the school is the best it for you, and how your specialist subject may benefit the school, You need to go on to say: how your experience is so far, what the school needs, how you feel you can improve a specific area the school may require improving (You'd get this from their last Ofsted report), and what specific attributes you'd bring to the school that no other perspective candidate would bring.

I found the personal part hard. It's you doing the best sales pitch of your life in order to hit all of the school's requirements without overselling yourself. While still managing to 'stand out from the crowd'. Then the presentation debate. Do I hand write the application, and show off my best, neatest, cursive script? Or do I word process it, so I can cram as many words in as possible, given the limited space and word count? If, like me, you write like a doctor in and your writing requires specialists (Usually six-year-old children) to decipher, then use the word process. Don't lose the job at the starting line.

Once submitted, you'll be informed via letter or telephone call if you have been successful and gained an interview. This is, of course, the next stop.

Interview Preparation

At the point you are informed of the interview time and date, you will also be given an extra piece of information. This is because a teaching interview is not as simple as being interviewed. A teaching interview takes all day. You will be given another tour of the school, meet the student council, carry-out a teaching task anywhere from thirty minutes to an hour in length, maybe have a spot of lunch, and then you will be interviewed. The whole process is drawn-out, extremely tiring, and something you need to be fresh and ready for.

Within the list of things that will take place on the day, it is the teaching task that holds the key to your success or failure. It is, after all, a teaching job. Your interview invite letter will take one of two forms. It will either state an area of the curriculum, year group, and a time. For example, 'We'd like you to teach a year 5 class an area of numeracy for thirty minutes'. Or it will be very specific about which area of the curriculum and elements to focus on. For example, 'We'd like you to teach a year 5 class a numeracy lesson, focussing on fractions for thirty minutes.

Now my opinion is the former of these two options is by far the less daunting than the latter! With an open brief, teaching numeracy to a year 5 class, you can showboat a whole range of your talents. You can go off curriculum, make sure all whistles and bells are included, and plan the best lesson you will ever teach.

You can plan a mixed ability activity, where everyone achieves the same outcome. You can go outside and be one with nature. You can include some addition, multiplication, and subtraction of percentages to fractions, or mixed fractions to whole numbers.

You can make up a shopping task or plan an end of year party where everyone's math knowledge comes together, and the mixed ability groups all support one another. At the end, everyone has participated, everyone has contributed, and you were the best teacher to enter that classroom all day. More than this, you can show engagement and achievement of the overall objective.

My experience was that with a very detailed brief, your lesson had to be specific and usually dictated by what time of the year it was and where the year group should be by that stage. If, for example it was early in the year, you may not want to go straight in with multiplication of mixed fractions, as this could be way above the knowledge and understanding of the class. Straight away you will lose them and subsequently your lesson will be blown.

On the other hand, if this is mid-year, or even later in the year, it could be expected that this is where the class should be, and you will have pitched the lesson correctly. Stretching the class on what they have already been taught earlier in the year. A very specific lesson brief usually indicates an area the children are struggling with, so your lesson plan needs to be precise about what they will learn, how they will learn it, and how the intended learning will be assessed at the end.

Not forgetting, of course, you will need to plan an activity for the less-able children, the mid-ability learners, the higher achievers, as well as any special educational needs the class may have. In addition, you will need to include a challenge and stretch activity for those higher attainers who may finish early, find resources for every planned activity, remembering that pen and paper activities don't suit everyone, so make something interactive, as well as plan a small, guided session for any teaching assistant who may be present during your lesson.

Finally, you need to make sure what you plan is relevant to the age group, up to date and includes a very clear introduction, starter activity, main session, and plenary. Not once forgetting the specifics set out in the letter, all within thirty minutes. The end result will be: you spend about three to four hours planning, looking for resources and extension activities, as well as making sure you include different learning styles, various assessment opportunities, and contingences for any errors. All for a class of children you have never met before and have no idea of how they behave or respond to new adults in their class. If that wasn't enough, you have no idea if you have support for the lesson, or if you'll fly solo!

Inevitably you will procrastinate more than you will plan. You will over think all possible scenarios until you end up with a faultless plan that covers all eventualities, and you are reasonably happy with. You have dotted al the I's, crossed all the T's, and ran through it in your head. This will be the plan that makes or breaks the lesson

In a non-teaching scenario, interviews can be pretty standard affairs. The day of your interview, you'll get up early and make sure everything is in place. A smart suit, some pieces of information about the company and, of course, well-rehearsed answers to 'Why do you want this job?', 'What can you bring to the role?' and 'Tell us about a time when...'

All being well, you will arrive on time, slightly sweaty but not noticeable. You'll find the right place you need to be make a great first impression. Soon you'll be called in for the interview of your life. You'll pull out some fantastic examples of evidence that you're the person for the job as you talk through your CV. And you'll also throw in some comments to show you researched the company and are really impressed with what they do.

A few questions may throw you off balance, but after a well-timed sip of water, you'll deal with these and be asked if you have any questions. Wracking your brain, you'll pull out a few questions while avoiding the obvious ones about salary, benefits, and holidays. Gain your responses, and the whole ordeal usually ends within the hour. All you need to do now is await the telephone call, which could potentially change your life. For now, at least.

The interview process to gain a teaching job is a far different experience than any other I have had before. Having worked in retail and finance, my first teaching interview was an odd and very new experience. The format of which hasn't changed throughout my career. Don't ever think a teaching interview is like any interview you have attended before.

Interview Day

A typical interview will take anywhere from 9.00 a.m. to 3.00 p.m., depending on your level of success throughout the day. Upon arriving at school, you will be given a rota for the day. The rota will contain a carousel of activities taking place throughout the day, where you will be slotted in at various times.

Then you will be shown to the staff room, or another room used very much like a holding pen. It is here you may see some familiar face. That's right, those people from the school visit all those weeks ago. Once again, today at least, these people are your rivals. There are six of you and only one job. In most cases, schools will aim to get six candidates in on the same day. Sometimes schools will interview over several days, or sometimes just allocate the one day for all candidates.

Be nice, but not too nice. Teaching interviews are the first kind of interview I ever attended where I got to check-out the competition, maybe plant a seed of doubt or two in the minds of the other candidates.

Once penned in, you may be offered a drink and then, depending on the rota time slots, there is lots of waiting around to do. A member of staff will come in and welcome you to the school and talk you through proceedings for the day. Here is where you are told only half of you will make the whole day. All lessons will be observed by the head, deputy head, and a governor or SLT member.

Then it will be decided the strongest candidates will be offered lunch, while the others will be thanked and sent home. You and the other candidates sit there clutching your pre-prepared lesson plans and resources like your life depends on them.

Sitting in the holding pen you will get to learn about your fellow candidates, whether you want to or not! Some have walked in, much like yourself, with various folders or wallets. Which you know encompasses their lesson plans and resources. Others have walked in clutching bags bulging with unseen objects and hidden gems, no doubt for the intended lesson.

Some have walked in, and you have already judged their outfit choices (Skirt too shirt, shoes too dirty, and 'really? That shirt with that jacket?') and decided they may not make the afternoon session. It is human nature that in a quiet room of people, someone will want to talk. Perhaps from nerves, or they're uncomfortable with the silence, or even an outgoing person. I was never that person.

Either way, they will want to break the silence and get some conversation flowing. Here is where your fellow competitors will begin to unfold before your very eyes. Often the silence is broken with 'So is everyone nervous?' or perhaps, 'Has everyone come very far?' There is nothing wrong with these ice-breaker questions. The fact is the icebreaker themselves should be rewarded for doing so, but that was never me. Rightly or wrongly, I was happy to just sit, absorb, and observe.

When people talk, specifically to strangers, they reveal a lot about themselves, either consciously or not. Answers to simple questions give you an idea if they are likeable or not. You can establish if this is their third or fifth interview, whether they are a parent or not, and if they drove here or got the bus. None of these things are relevant, though. What you really want to know is: are you already a teacher and what have you planned according to the lesson brief? More specifically, does your plan sound better than mine?

Sitting back and just listening, giving the odd nod or grunt here and there, is all well and good. And can give you lots of information. You can listen to who already teaches and what school they are at.

Possibly useful information if you don't get the job today. You can work out how much time and effort were put into today's lesson plan, establishing yourself if you have planned enough or not. If asked, people will reveal in detail their 'killer element' or 'surprise fact' they will pull out in the lesson. Who knows, if you like the ideas and you are before them, you can steal it and add it in somewhere yourself. You quickly glance at the rota and look for their names and order they are teaching in.

****

So, you've sat back and taken in all of this information. Now you process who you think your competition is for the day. If you are an ECT at this stage, this can be a disheartening time. In a room full of six, you and one other are ECT's and the other four are experienced teachers. Do you worry, or just reassure yourself that you're ok because you are one of the cheapest prospects in the room? If, however, you have some teaching experience under your belt, you need more information. Which means joining in the conversation. This is harder than can be imagined as very often, I was the only male in the room.

My experiences have been that there are fewer males in primary schools than females. And while this can be an advantage in a room full of mixed aged females, joining in a conversation can be hard. The conversation evolves and you're asked a question, allowing you to join in. The question is about your lesson plan, which you want to keep closely guarded, so you try to be cautious with your response. While responding politely, you give nothing away. Unlike the experienced teacher sitting across from you who can't wait to boast about her 'tried and tested content' and 'inevitable outcomes'. All said, of course, with the aim of unbalancing everyone in the room.

Not me, I was always confident with my plan. Conversations will unfold about who came from where, how nervous, or not, everyone is and one-by-one, candidates will be lead away for their tour or their meeting with the student council. Slowly the room will empty.

Your name will eventually be called. It's your turn to be paraded around the school and meet the student council. This is never really a joyful experience. Over-confident children asking questions you'd rather not answer. You straighten yourself up and try to look interested while you are being shown around the school for the second time. Next, you'll be taken into a room where four children of various ages each sit with a piece of paper in front of them. While I appreciate the school's efforts to include their children in the selection process, I would be horrified to think that they have the deciding word on who they want their new teacher to be!

Each child asks a series of question, ranging from: Are you strict? What are your views on homework? Are you married? And what new thing will you bring to the school? From memory, my worst experience of this scenario was when a child asked me to tell them a joke. Four faces, ages ranging from eight to ten, all staring at me, waiting for my response. Sweat dripping from every pour, I was wracking my brain for child friendly, non-offensive, non-sexist jokes. Did I know any? I took a sip of water and then bingo! My killer jokes: 'What's brown and sticky? A stick!' Some chuckles, so I throw another one in, 'What's orange and sounds like a parrot? A carrot!' More chuckles, so my last one 'What do you call a fish with no eyes (I's)? A fsh!' (This joke works better orally than it does written). Four children sitting in front of me dissolve into fits of giggles – success!

Back to the holding pen to join some, while others have dispersed for their lesson or their tours. As you sit someone will ask, 'How was that?' assuming I have just taught. 'Ok', I reply. 'They liked my jokes, so if nothing else I made some kids laugh today'. Mrs. Experienced Teacher sitting across the way reminds me, 'Don't call them kids, staff won't like this, they are children'. Yeah, thanks for the reminder!

Finally, you will be called to deliver your lesson. You will be led to a classroom where twenty plus children await your instructions, and you notice four unoccupied seats at the back of the class. You're given a few minutes to set-up and get yourself ready, during which time all the class are looking at you and are already beginning to become unsettled. You place a copy of your lesson plan on each empty seat, prepare your visuals, and sort your resources into ability piles. It's not obvious, at this stage which tables are which ability, and you pray for some indication. At this stage a child shouts, 'I'm bored!' while his classmates giggle uncontrollably. Good, you've just established the less able group!

You write your name on the board and greet the class. Five adults casually walk in, four taking their seats and your lesson plan at the back, while the fifth adult sits in the middle of the class. Your best guess is that must be the teaching assistant, and they have possibly sat with the mid-ability group. In an ideal world, you'd grab a minute and ask them to identify the groups, to which they willingly oblige. These experiences being observed are rarely ideal.

Observed interview lessons can go two ways, depending on many factors. Mainly your nerves and the response from the kids, sorry, children! If you approach your planned lesson with confidence, the only factor that could let you down is the children. In my experience, the observers know you can't account for children's responses. but will take note on how you deal with them.

Worst case scenario? Your lesson starts and immediately you know the class has no idea what you're talking about. (Pitched too high) Or they breeze through your planned activities with relative ease. (Pitched too low). I have experienced of both of these scenarios. You wrack your brain for extension questions and activities to ease the tension, but nothing comes, so you plough on with the plan.

To add to this, the interactive whiteboard does not want to play. And while this is not your fault, it does add more stress to the session. You run behind time because several questions come up that required much explanation, the TA does not understand your activity, and two boys at the back just won't be quiet and have distracted you from the moment you said 'hello'. All said and done, you run out of time. This is always signalled by the observers standing up and leaving the room. And the children are left with an unfinished piece of work with no clue what they were asked to achieve. On the plus side, they will remember you!

Best case scenario? Your lesson goes as smooth as silk. You have gauged their interest with your introduction activity, managing to ask enough engaging assessment questions without being disrupted. The TA has already begun the planned activity and their table is buzzing. You have sat with the lower attaining children, and they are lost in your activity, hanging on every word. In the middle of the class the other children are busy problem solving, with just the right amount of chat, you can overhear relevant questions and discussion. You pause, mini-plenary time.

A quick assessment question to all groups demonstrates they are on task, fully engaged. and understand what to do next. So, you continue. You are aware four bodies are moving around the room and sitting at different tables. You don't panic because you just assessed, and all is good. Eventually, you leave your group, sit with the other tables for thirty seconds and decide no intervention is required.

Finally, you ask the whole class to stop using non-verbal communication, and peace descends. You use your planned assessment questions to establish what each table has achieved and make note on your plans. Referring to the learning objective you ask for a thumbs up / thumbs down vote and leave the room, heading back to the holding pen.

Back in the holing pen, it's almost lunchtime and you know the hammer will fall on half the group. If you produced a best-case scenario, you sit back with confidence you'll be eating fishfingers and chips with children in about half an hour's time. If you delivered a worst-case scenario lesson, you're already packing your things and wondering if you'll get home in time for this afternoons Countdown. The holding room is now buzzing with everyone sharing their lesson experiences.

You overhear the successes and failures of the others and find out that Mrs. Experienced Teacher had a nightmare, to your sheer joy! Listening in, you find out the bulging bag contained a stuffed animal, a trumpet, and a top-hat. You wonder how on earth these were used in a numeracy lesson. Out of nothing but nosiness, you're asked, 'How did it go?' Depending on the scenario lesson, you revel in your success, or you share a tale of IT failures, disruptive and disrespectful children, and an incompetent TA. Thus, making sure when you leave before lunch the remaining candidates feel sorry for you, rather than chuckle at your nightmare.

Having polished off the local authorities best fishfingers and chips, there is more waiting, though the day is nearly done. The holding pen is far quieter now as 50% of the candidates have been sent home.

One shock decision, one obvious decision, and Mrs. Experienced Teacher, to your joy. The final obstacle is the actual interview part of the day. After what seems like a lifetime of small talk with the other candidates, your call for the interview arrives. From the holding pen to the head teacher's office feels like the green mile. Yet here you are, your first opportunity to talk to the lesson observers and make your next impression.

The Interview

In my experience, the interview will always open with introductions around the room. Who's who sat around the table, and this is then followed with something like, 'Thank-you for spending the day here, meeting the children and thank-you for your lesson, which we all enjoyed'. Part of this must be true or you'd be at home now, slouched on the sofa working your way through Countdown.

Next follows, 'So, how do you think your lesson went?' I have even been on interview panels where this was the first question. This is your opportunity to reflect on how you felt you did in accordance with the brief and the lesson plan you submitted. Here you must be a pleasant mixture of humble, informative, reflective, and analytical. They don't want to hear how great you were, how perfectly executed your plan was, and how pleased you were that everything went well. They are looking for *why* you think things went well, *how* could you improve, and *where*. What would you do differently had you known the class dynamics?

Beyond the lesson dissection, you will then be asked about all things you. What is your experience? Why did you decide on teaching? What are your strengths? What is your inner leg measurement? And what turns you on? (I may have made some of those up) Basically, this is a test. Can you remember, word for word, what you wrote in your personal statement all those weeks ago?

Next you will be told all about the school. How proud they all are to work there, how wonderful and aspirational all the staff are, and how well-behaved all the children are. It will be highlighted to you that if chosen for the role, you will join a very special club of teachers and helpers who all feel so much pride at working for the school. While this may all be true, I have found the thicker it is laid on the less true it actually is. Good schools speak for themselves.

Each person at the table in turn will then ask you a set of questions. Usually about four questions each. These range from: 'Tell me a time when you went over and above for a child', 'Explain what you would do if a child disclosed something to you', to 'Can you tell us when something didn't go according to plan, and what you did about it?'. Each question is carefully designed to test your knowledge, experience, and what you work like under pressure.

The interview will usually end with, 'Do you have any questions for us?' I mean, does anyone actually say no? This is your opportunity to show them you have listened and absorbed everything about the school. You chance to pull out a question which will bring a smile to each face as they realise you and only you are perfect for this role.

Finally, you will be asked, 'If you were offered the job, would you accept?' I mean, really? 'No. No I don't want the job, thank you. I disliked your fishfingers, your classrooms are too small, your IT is pre-dinosaur era, and I have seen several children already who make me feel physically sick!'

'Yes', you reply. 'I'd really like the opportunity to work here and be part of this community'.

You leave, get back in the car, and heave a huge sigh of relief. And now the waiting begins. Unlike most jobs, you will find out that very day if you have or have not been successful. Usually, the call will come before 6 p.m. My experience has taught-me this: if the head teacher calls you, you have got the job. Spray the champagne, kick back and enjoy the summer, you are a teacher! If the governor, or member of SLT calls you then unfortunately on this occasion you were not successful, and so begins the analysis.

You can be given feedback on the phone, ranging from a minor detail in your teaching to something you said in interview. It may even be the case they had an internal applicant that was successful in acquiring the role. In which case, why did you waste six hours of my time if they were getting the job anyway? If no feedback is given, you are invited to call back or write in for written confirmation. Either way, it's back to the drawing board and the whole cycle begins again. Good luck!

It cannot go unmentioned the sheer joy and pleasure felt when the call comes through, and you have secured the role. All the preparation, research, and time spent preparing that killer lesson pale into insignificance. Because you, and only you, walked into that school, taught the best you could, and blew away the interview panel. There is no feeling like securing your first teaching role. Fresh out of university, graduation day looming, you secure your first job and the world around you seems like such a nicer place. The training, the debt, the late nights studying all paid off. As anyone who teaches will tell you securing a teaching role is no mean feat. When it does happen, you know you were the best of the best on that day. Like I said, securing that first teaching job, there's no feeling like it.

The ECT Year

To make you the best teacher you can be, we will offer personal guidance and support

As a child, I never knew a new teacher from an old teacher. Not in terms of years old, just in terms of time spent in my school. Sure, there were times when you'd go to a lesson and an unfamiliar face greeted you in class. Or times when the headteacher would step in to take a lesson in the absence of your regular teacher. These occasions were infrequent and even when they did happen, they didn't disrupt the learning, we just got on with it. Of course, I recall new teachers in school. It was very common to start a new year and meet a new teacher. It was never questioned if the person standing at the front of the class knew their stuff or not. It would be inconceivable to think that this wasn't the best person to do the job. As a child, a pupil and a learner, this person was the teacher and as such, was there to help guide me through my learning.

If all goes to plan, you will secure your first teaching job in your final year as a student. Assuming you take the three-year teaching degree and not the lesser relevant short-cut, the P.G.C.E. All being well you will leave university fully employed in your first post, and already submitting a holiday request to attend your graduation ceremony. I was actually questioned by my first ever head teacher if I felt it was essential that I took the day off to attend my graduation ceremony!

As graduation day arrives, you'll already be sharing stories of class size, year groups, staffroom gossip, and workload. Despite all of this, you know that by time you walk up on stage and collect your fake, plastic scroll, you are a fully-fledged, gainfully employed, pillar of the community and the last three years were all worth it. You'll pose for your obligatory graduation picture, hug and kiss the parents. And then, once they slip £100 into your sweaty palms for doing them so proud, you'll ditch the old folks and go celebrate your achievements with one last university standard, monumental blow out of drink and recklessness. If you were clever, you will have booked the following day off and revel in the memory of the previous night, knowing that it will be the last one you have for some time. Onward and upwards for now, you are a teacher! I was lucky that my graduation was on a Friday, so I didn't need to upset my new head by asking for two days off!

First Impressions

Before you start as the new 'Mr', 'Mrs', or 'Miss' at the new school, hopefully you have manged to arrange some observation days where you go in and visit the school you have just landed your job at. Two things to remember here: Firstly, this is vital. These days will be your first insight (Beyond the interview, which was months ago, and you don't even remember what you said) into what your new place of work will be like. It will give you the valuable information you need to know about expectations, standards, daily routines, your new work environment, classroom, and colleagues.

During this time, you will be introduced to your new work mates, your first opportunity to make a good impression. You'll more than likely spend time with your new headteacher and your ECT mentor. You'll be allowed to meet all the adults in the school by spending time in the staffroom. You'll be questioned and scrutinised by everyone you meet, because everyone will want to know who you are, where you are from, what subject you studied, and what year group you have got. The last one of these questions will give you a real insight into your prospective class. The reaction of your new colleagues will be the best gauge of what your new class will be like. As you announce, 'year 3' or 'year 5', the faces of those asking will set out the path of your first year in teaching.

You recall the job advertisement being for key stage two and there was mention in the interview of year 5e, but what year group are you taking? As your first observation day ends, your brain will be filled with questions, new names and faces, and your arms full of folders containing policies and procedures.

It is more likely your second visit will be the schools shuffle-up day, also known as the meet the teacher day. Here is your first opportunity to meet your new class. In advance of doing so you should have prepared a nice activity which allows the children to tell you something about themselves. Which you can then etch to memory and remember for the next academic year.

At some point you will be escorted into your new classroom where you automatically start to check out wall display space, table and chair alignment, whiteboard position and view from the window. You're introduced as 'The school's new teacher and your teacher for next year'. The door will close and here is your first real taste of life at your new school. You'll bid the class a polite hello and introduce yourself. Immediately someone will laugh at your surname, and instantly link it to some sort of cartoon or comedy character. The class will laugh, as will you before calming everyone down. (Note to self, remember the name of said child and ensure he 'gets his' on day one)

By the end of your time there you will have been asked: 'Are you married?' 'What's your first name?' 'What car do you drive?' 'Have you ever taught before?' 'Do you like blue?' As well as a whole other barrage of random questions. Inevitably, you will leave with a handful of completed and uncompleted activities, no idea of which child was called what, crayon or pen on your nice new suit, and the aromatic odour of child farts fresh in your nostrils.

The second, and probably most important thing to remember is everything you see, everyone you talk to, and everything you do is fake! Smoke and mirrors. Not real life. Everyone in school, including the children, knew you were coming. Everyone was prepped and told in advance that everyone needed to make a good impression. Just like any impending local authority or Ofsted visit, everything you experienced was planned and put in place to create a good impression. The chocolate biscuits in the staffroom – purchased the morning of your visit. The nice, clean school embossed mugs – taken out of the cupboard normally reserved for governors' meetings. The fresh smelling staff toilets – cleaned by the caretaker just before you arrived. Even the children you spent time with – all pre-warned to be on their best behaviour for their new teacher. The same children, who by the way, are now snitching on one another for asking, 'what's your name' and blaming each other for the farting!

Just like the day of the school visit and following interviews, the school, the staff, and the children were all showboated to be the best impression of the school. Why? Because the head wants you to feel and think you made the right choice, and that this is the school for you. Don't ever lose sight of the fact your observation days will more likely be at the end of term. This means that underneath the veil of smoke, teachers are knackered, the children lost interest weeks ago, and everyone is counting down to the summer holidays.

Don't ever let anyone tell you that being a newly qualified teacher is easy! This year will be your most challenging, full-throttle introduction to teaching you will ever encounter. You've had the summer to prepare, even managed to go back to school and prepare bright, colourful and child-friendly displays for your new classroom. Your head is equally full of ideas, and you are ready to start. You've bid a fond farewell to your liquid buddies Jack (Daniels) and Morgan (Spiced Rum) and, remembering all of the lessons you taught in your final placement school, you are ready to take the bull by the horns. You are, after all, a teacher.

What to Expect

As a ECT your school is expected to provide you with a ECT mentor. This will be someone who holds qualified teacher status (QTS) and is an experienced member of staff. Their role will be to help guide and steer you through your first year (Reduced national curriculum teaching), observe you, and give feedback for any areas of improvement, and to help with any scenario new to you in your new role. In some cases, you will be introduced to this person on one of the observation days. They will be kind, caring, and compassionate to all your fears and have a structured plan set out for your first term.

My own experience of a ECT mentor was indeed very different to this. From day one he was resentful of yet another responsibility, made it clear to me that this mentor role was part of his own CPD, and he had not mentored anyone else before. But assured me, 'We will make it up as we go along'. His own arrogance allowed him to tell me what a great teacher he was, yet his own ego failed to tell me he was overloaded, but too scared to tell the head teacher. No coincidence then, that I didn't meet this person on one of the planned visit days.

In your ECT year you will be given a folder containing the ECT and QTS standards. This will become your bible for the next academic year. Everything you do, plan, and say will be in accordance with these standards. As your year progresses, you will need these standards to be signed off by your mentor for you to achieve the elusive qualified teacher standard (QTS) goal. This folder will be the guide that provides you and your mentor with a step-by-step road map as to where you need to end up and how you will get there.

As you begin your journey any worries, concerns, achievements, and successes will all be recorded and kept in your folder as evidence of your progression. It's worth noting, any entries in there should be agreed with your mentor. They should be a two-way dialogue and not a diary that your mentor makes up, completes on your behalf, or uses as a yard stick to beat you with!

More likely than not, your first day will be a planned inset day. An opportunity to delay the start of term by another day and / or an opportunity to receive vital input into new school initiatives, become familiar with the school improvement plan, as well as what assessment process the school will follow for the core subjects. As a ECT it is also an opportunity to meet the staff, again in a more relaxed and realistic manner. You may experience the sheer hell of being asked to introduce yourself to the whole team in either the hall or the staffroom. Feeling like a newbie at alcoholics anonymous, you get up and spout out some unrehearsed blurb which contains your name, age, experience, and marital status. Sitting back down, you feel a total clown and less relaxed than you were on your first prostate examination. By time the day ends, you have met your teaching assistant. Who will either be full of joy at the prospect of working with a new teacher with new ideas and a new approach, or they will be full of resentment at the thought of having to hand hold the newbie. Also, you will have fine tunned your class displays and have a list of class and school rules in hand.

The ECT Teaching Experience

As my first real teaching day arrived, I felt like a bag of excitable nerves. Arriving early, new work suit freshly ironed, shoes polished, and head full of ideas, I made the final changes to my desks and felt ready to go. I had nice, fresh, blank displays ready to be filled as the weeks progressed, and I made sure the class rules and school rules were clearly displayed. Readily prepared was a register of my class, as well as my name and date clearly shown on the board. All the children's drawers and pegs were labelled with nicely cut, laminated name labels, and the lunchtime trolley was empty outside my door. Here I was, ready for day one.

As the clock got closer to 8.45 a.m., a calm descended on the school. As I popped my head outside my door, I heard nothing, a deathly silence. Suddenly, the outer door of my class swung open, and my new teaching assistant screamed,—'Your class is outside waiting to come in!'

As I collected my jacket and moved outside, I saw every class teacher in the school standing proudly in front of nice, neat lines of children. My class was in some sort of zig-zag shaped line, all talking and wondering where their teacher was. I raised my hand and asked for silence before leading everyone inside. Mistake number one – not being outside in time – noted by every teacher and child in school. Not the things you learn in university or on placement.

The first time you stand in front of your own class is… Well not dissimilar to standing in front of a firing squad, I imagine. All eyes on you, just waiting for an instruction. Waiting for the words of wisdom to pour out of your newly qualified mouth You, on the other hand, stand there gazing. Forgetting everything you need to do, to say, and just gaze.

In your best, most well-rehearsed and non-threatening voice you ask for silence. You're heard, but not quite enough. So, you repeat, except louder. Time to deploy the secret weapon, a raised hand with five fingers, each folding down in turn with the expectation the class will be stone dead silent as the last finger falls. Eventually, the children will quiet down, and you know the register needs to be taken.

The register, be it electronic or handwritten, is your first most important job. It's almost a rite of passage that you will pronounce a child's name incorrectly, maybe more than one. Today, children's names range from David to Dynasty, Charlie to Chardonnay, and Billie to Bhindra. It's hard to know, unless sounded out phonetically, how to pronounce an unfamiliar name so it's no surprise you'll get it wrong. I did this on many occasions. To add to the list of errors on day one, you need to add the registration key.

As you stare at the registration of names, you have no idea how to acknowledge attendance, absence, sickness, packed lunch, or school dinners. The best thing to do here, given you haven't been informed, there is no obvious code and it's a brand-new register, is to make an informed guess. '/' will indicate attendance. 'A' will indicate absence, 'P' will equal packed lunch. 'S' will indicate sickness. 'D' will equal dinners. Easy. Register done you have several small bags of money pushed into your hands. It's not payday already and these guys are too young to be offering bribes, so you assume it's lunch money. All the cash is gathered in, placed into a clear folder, and sent with a sensible looking child to the office. This child will later turn out to be an untrustworthy thief who steals lunch money from the register. Something else not taught in university or on your many placements.

The first day of term as a ECT is a minefield. You've already been told the first few days are important, getting to know you and your class days. You've planned some activities loosely based around some kind of learning in the hope the children will relax and ease into their first few days. What you will notice, very early on, is how relentless children can be. The constant noise, questioning, bickering, and total lack of context. Not to mention the ever-present smell of farts.

Despite your best planned seating arrangements, someone somewhere won't be able to sit with someone else. Despite the fact all you are doing is self-portrait information painting, one girl won't be able to sit across from another because their mothers had a coffee spilt over them by their ex-husband's brother, who is the uncle of one of the girls, who once burnt down a tree and was arrested and the other girl saw it all and filmed it on her phone and uploaded it to Facebook! By the end of your first day, all you will have achieved here is moving each of the girls several times. Only to find neither of them get on with anyone, or they are both related to every other child in the class.

Your first day will be full of mistakes, miscommunications, and the unknown. Wrong names are just the start of things. You'll soon find out that the register codes you devised were all wrong. As a result, the receptionist has no idea who is here, who is absent, who has packed lunch, and who has free school meals. You'll find out, 'That's not the way we write the date, Sir', from several helpful voices.

You'll become aware there is a warning system in place for discipline and, no matter what the event, who the individual is and no matter what the offence, everyone goes through the same system. First a warning: You're on my radar, but essentially this is an empty threat. Second warning: Still on my radar, but now I'm annoyed. Final warning: This could be removal of the child to another class or sending to the head. You'll learn that hot drinks are a fantasy as no teacher worth their own reputation ever drinks a drink which exceeds lukewarm at best. To add to this, you'll swiftly learn that all drinks must be in a school approved, sealed lid cup. This is usually a lesson learnt on the way out of the staffroom and delivered from the head – Great start!

Finally, you'll learn (Should you ever be in the position of working in a Catholic school) that making the sign of the cross does not go down well with the wrong hand and in the wrong direction. (How was I supposed to know?)

As your ECT year progresses, the lessons you'll learn and the mistakes you'll make will come thick and fast. The list is endless and as the saying goes, 'You don't know what you don't know, until you need to know it'. Your ECT year will open your eyes to the harsh realisation that your three-year degree course prepared you for the theory of teaching, but not the actual practical reality of the job.

Some mistakes are forgivable and expected – see above and add on ten more. Other mistakes will send shivers down your spine and may scare you a little. These may include: finding out your experience of methods for short division / long multiplication are not up to scratch, despite best efforts you cannot be expected to speak both Spanish and French fluently, as well as being constantly reminded (usually by your teaching assistant) you cannot be and must not be the children's friend.

Inevitably, there will be the genuine mistakes that make you feel like you want the earth to open up and swallow you. Everyone will make them, not everyone will be found out, but those who do and who are will be such better teachers for having had the experience(s). Mistakes are part of learning and growing. In teaching it's more than likely this growing phase will happen in front of thirty children, other adults and / or your superiors. You'll spell a word wrong, an obvious word. Normally this is forgivable, except when you project it onto thirty children, and it's picked up by your line manager. You'll forget all of the conversations about being the adult and find yourself arguing with a child, not reasoning or rationalising, but actually arguing. Despite all best efforts, this will be heard, or seen, by another adult. Or worse still, a child. At some point the mask will slip, all be it momentarily.

You won't know it's going to happen. You'll do all you can to make sure it doesn't. but the sheer weight of responsibility, stress, and long hours will take its toll. When and where this happens is the huge unknown. For some it could be tears in class, in the staffroom, or worse still, in private. For others it could be far worse, but more obvious. Pent up frustrations resulting in a random swear word being verbalised in class (Shocker, our teacher knows words we use), a book or folder being hurled to the floor, or random table, or the loudest, most unprovoked scream ever.

Despite all justification for any, or all of these, it's never expected, never received well, and never acceptable. To make matters worse, you could have a head teacher who has no time, patience, or even concern for you. If, like me, you are faced with this, your ECT year will be nothing short of hell. Teaching is like no other job. In other jobs some or all of these examples are forgivable, expected, and warranted. In teaching some or all of these examples are worthy of disciplinary action. In your ECT year, they could cost you your job and career.

I made many mistakes in my ECT year. Every single one of them flagged up to an unsupportive mentor who then took his worries to a black-hearted, cold and miserable head teacher. I argued with a child, I argued with a parent, I even argued with my teaching assistant. To add to this, I called children the wrong names, marked using the wrong colour pens, and a whole bunch of other mistakes, too. The important things to remember are: You are human, and no one died because you marked in green and not pink. And in the absolute worst case, you leave (I did!). I decided my development was not the concern of my chosen school, and if I was ever going to be a good teacher this was not the place for me. I resigned and left at Easter. Zero emotion from my head or mentor and only the backing of some colleagues and the local authority. It was a huge step. However, with determination and experience of what not to do, I found a wonderful village school, where not only did

I complete my ECT year, but I was signed off as a qualified teacher. All within the first year.

Despite the pressures, the hours and the demands, the first year in teaching can be one of the most rewarding years you'll ever have in the job. You cannot and will not know every element of the job. The nerves, the lack of experience, and the wide-eyed approach to everything is evident. You can't hide it. In the right school, with the right staff, all of this will be rewarded.

Most schools will welcome a newly qualified teacher with open arms. In preparation for their arrival, systems, people and processes will be put in place. A fully trained, experienced mentor will be briefed and ready upon arrival. They will welcome, calm and reassure the ECT, ready to help and answer all questions. An experienced, friendly, knowledgeable, and understanding teaching assistant will introduce you to routines, procedures, and expectations. Staff will pull you under their wing and rest your fears, making you feel like part of the team from day one. A good headteacher will allocate you and your mentor joint non-contact time and agreed catch-up sessions for feedback, observations, and development opportunities.

Regular meetings with your head and senior leaders will become routine and you will soon develop a sense of belonging and team spirit. These schools will nurture and develop a ECT as a sign of their commitment to retaining them for years to come. Not just the initial year. As the ECT these scenarios need to be embraced. In no other year will you get this level of support, this amount of non-contact time or the safety net of, 'But I'm new and didn't know'. This first year can ignite the fire in your belly and fan the flames of passion to drive you towards your retirement. Your introduction to teaching can be the best start to any job you've ever had. Nurtured, developed, and given the motivation by those around you, the ECT year can be the most rewarding thing you ever decided to do. Don't be fooled though, it will be exhausting.

The Staffroom

Just imagine the staffroom as your own haven

As I child I always remember the staffroom being a magical place of mystery and intrigue. The heavy doors blocking the view of any pupil. On the rare occasion the door swung open, billows of smoke pouring out from inside, an obvious and heavy smoke cloud lingering in mid-air. This was before it was unacceptable to smoke indoors! Hushed hustle and bustle of teacher's discussions creeping from within the secret room. I recall once, and only once, knocking on the door to ask for a specific teacher. My reward? I was bellowed at by my then deputy head teacher to promptly, 'Get outside' unless I wanted detention that evening!

I don't ever recall seeing the inside of a staff room as a child. Yes, there were glances through windows trying to make out the silhouettes of who was who by process of illumination of who was on playground duty. The staffroom was always a place for adults and only adults. Children approached at their own risk and consequences always followed should you be brave enough.

From recollection, the closest permitted space for children was a desk parallel to the entrance. This was today's equivalent of the time out room or naughty step. A table for the child who disrupted class, showed up late, or forgot their homework. A single table carefully positioned so every teacher passing could pause long enough to tut, drop their glasses, and shake their head, or just stop to say your name aloud in disgust.

Why was that room so intriguing to us children back then?

Staffrooms in today's modern schools are a very different place. Gone is the permanent, low hanging cloud of cigarette smoke. Gone is the stench of coffee slowly brewing away in the pot. No more are the staffrooms shut off from pupils and visitors. Gone is the mystery.

No, today's staffrooms are very different places indeed. The modern staffroom has become an extension of the classroom. Clean, tidy, places of work kept crisp and perfect where everything has a place.

The dishwasher churns away as the wall mounted water heater boils away with carefully placed, neatly laminated health and safety sign on show. All kettles have been banished to the depths of the under-sink cupboard. We can't have trailing leads at the risk someone could catch it and accidently, spill its contents-and risk burning themselves, can we? Not forgetting that the 'someone' is a degree educated, intellectual adult!

Meticulous notice boards, with well-designed timetables and upcoming events remind the teacher that life does not stop in their communal meeting place. The largest notice board in the whole school is carefully divided into days of the week and weeks of term. Each space containing lists of who takes which assembly, who takes which staff meeting and not forgetting, who has and has not paid this terms tea money. Don't ever be that person!

The seats are carefully arranged so everyone can see everyone else, because God forbid, we don't all stare uncomfortably into one another's eyes as we eat or make an agonising point at the staff meeting. The downside is it's always one or two seats short of the actual number of staff members. Within the cluster of chairs are carefully placed child friendly seats ready for the imminent arrival of the 'needy child' who just needs 'speak to Sir' or 'needs Miss for something'. Chairs ready for children to come in, sit down and feel safe.

No longer are staff room places teachers can be found relaxing with a coffee and a cig while the children run around the playground for twenty minutes. No, teachers can be found in the staffroom at any given time of the day, and day of the week by anyone taking the time to look. P.P.A is dedicated time-teachers are allocated outside of teaching time to do exactly that – plan, prepare, and assess. Usually, this time is taken in the staff room. A quiet, relaxing, well-resourced area for teachers to work when not in class...or so it would seem.

Staffrooms have become a second classroom space. The upsides to this being; everything on hand, including the coffee making facilities, for a peaceful and productive PPA session.

The downsides are you have to put up with the lunchtime supervisors turning up forty minutes in advance, for their daily catch-up. As well as the child from your class sent to you as punishment for not working with the cover teacher, who is currently taking your class adhering to your carefully planned lesson plan and not daring to use their own initiative.

Overall, staffrooms have lost their privacy, alure, and mystery. These have all been abandoned along with the thick clouds of cigarette smoke and wheezy coughing teachers of old, never to be seen again.

Having said this, the staffroom can be one of the best places in a school, especially if you're an ECT or RQT. They can be warm, welcoming, and tranquil places in the right school. If you are lucky enough to find a school who value their staffroom and do treat it as a 'teacher only zone', you will find some of the nicest colleagues and friends tucked away in its four walls. A place full of laughter, friendly gossip, support, and good coffee. These are truly the gems which make every break time and lunchtime worthy of at least a ten-minute sit down.

Parent's Evening

*Make sure every effort is made to see
all parents*

As a child my memories of parents evening are vague. Did I go with my parents? Was I asked to wait outside? I know they went, but I don't recall the logistics of attending myself. Maybe they didn't happen. Was everything just sent home as a report? At best, my memory recall is that my parents attended after school and I stayed at home, who knows? I asked my mum; her memory is vaguer than mine!

My childhood reports, however, I do recall. Single slips of paper divided into subjects and each subject getting a grade awarded A-F.

Today's parent evenings are, to say the least, very structured in some schools I have worked in, almost to military standards. A list of time slots goes on all access points to the classroom, as well as a copy being handed in to the office. Parents are asked to sign up in a slot no longer than ten minutes, anywhere from 3.30 p.m. – 6.30 p.m. Because a teacher's working days isn't already long enough! Parents are also asked to consider if they have younger / older siblings not to make appointments back-to-back and consider the time it takes to travel from one teacher to another.

Inevitably the first sign up is either bang on 3.30 p.m. So, straight from the home time bell into a parent meeting. OR, more annoyingly, the last slot of the day, 6.20 p.m. – 6.30 p.m. The latter means you'll still be sat there at 6.45 p.m., trying to strategically sweep the parent out the door as if you're depending on the Olympic gold medal for curling!

Weeks pass, there are still slots on the sign-up sheet not filled, and you are gently reminded by the head to chase the parents who haven't signed up. When are you expected to make these calls? Oh, just casually in your break-time between getting the next lesson ready and finishing this morning's cold cup of coffee. Lunch-time, once you've tided the room, prepared resources for the last two lessons, and dealt with a minor scuffle which the lunchtime supervisors have walked away from after gas lighting by shouting and screaming at all involved. Or perhaps when school finishes, once you've seen out all the children, waited with the perennial straggler whose parent always shows up twenty minutes late, gathered together all the stray pencils and ruler from the floor, and finally managed to finish your coffee from 12.45 p.m.

Calling parents is always interesting. Most of the time the teacher will leave a message, as no doubt the parent sees the words 'school' on their mobile phone display and decides to reject or ignore the call. Specifically, during school hours, as to be honest 'my child is the school's problem and not mine' during this time. On the rare occasion the parent does pick up it's either defence mode or panic mode straight away.

Eventually all parents will have been chased and the time sheet will slowly begin to fill up. Despite best efforts the parent of 'that child' will dodge all efforts to attend or try to just grab you before school one day, yeah right! I've learnt over the years a trick to keeping sane. While in an ideal world your parent meetings would be ten minutes back-to-back where everyone shows up and sticks to the allocated time slot, we do not live in a perfect world. So, the exact opposite of this happens.

A trick to negate some of the stress of the evening: The phantom parent time slot. On the day of the meetings, or perhaps the day before, fill in a ten-minute slot with the name of a parent you know won't show up. While I agree this is somewhat a game of devil's advocate as that parent may actually think they put their name down and feel compelled to turn up, it does buy a ten-minute rest period where you can sneak off for a cup of coffee. Or just sit and take the time to bring your heart rate down and remember your breathing pattern. Not wholly ethical, but usually essential.

As the two back-to-back evenings approach, you are reminded to ensure all books are displayed, marked and up to date, containing a wide mix of positive and supportive feedback. As well as ensuring there is sufficient verbal feedback between yourself and the child. Where possible the teacher should also be aware how many good work awards and star of the week certificates every child has had. Valuable information, eh?

This leads to inevitable panic as the reality sets in that you haven't marked your topic book for three weeks, your French books haven't been marked all term, and the sessions your PPA teacher takes haven't seen a green or pink pen all year! Panic mode sets in and speed marking begins! The last session of the day before each evening becomes a feedback to marking session, while you reassure all children 'This is normal' and 'Of course I look at your books. It's just some don't really need marking'.

Parents evening arrives. You're jacked up on stale coffee and just pray the odd parent or two doesn't show. You're already looking forward to the phantom appointment halfway through. The books are all ready, marked, up to date with sufficient pupil / teacher feedback comments.-You have a carefully constructed sheet prepared showing all children's previous assessment levels, as well as their predicted levels. Your coffee cup is at arm's length out of sight, you're ready to go.

A quick glance outside your classroom and several children, some yours, some the teacher's next door and others you've never seen before, are already throwing books and Lego around the communal work areas. Parents must be here. The walk to the hallway feels like the green mile. A desk is placed around the outside of the hall, and you spot your name. Shuffling carefully across the hall, arms full of children's trays, a parent accosts you with a myriad of questions. You haven't sat down yet and realise you're already running behind time.

The first few appointments are the best you'll ever be on that night. The questions asked are fresh, as are your responses, you are alert (Caffeine enthused) and enjoying feeding back some positive comments about your loveliest children. Parents are on time, some have even glanced through the books and made comments on the neatness of their child's work, as well as the growing trust and relationship in the teacher / student feedback. Missing those two-music lessons at the end of the day was worth it then!

The evening slowly trudges on, and the second wave of the evening begins. It's ok though, only three more parents and then your phantom parent coffee break. You gaze around at your colleagues. They, too, have the same look of despair on their faces. Some are busy with orderly lines forming, others are sitting, tapping pens and anxiously looking at their watches. You look at your sign-up sheet and realise the next two meetings will be a challenge. One is a parent you always see every day at the door, twice a day. What can you tell them that they don't already know? What can they possibly hear that you haven't discussed every day since term began? Assessment levels, that's it! This one should be nice and short then, a quick, 'Hey, nice to see you, again. As you know, all is well...blah, blah!' Quick chat about predicted levels, all done. 'See you tomorrow at the door, usual time'. The other, now this is a very different story and possibly endangers your phantom parent slot. Nope. It won't happen. You've sat there all night, you deserve that ten-minute break, you will get it! The two parents show up. Dammit. The first one on time, too.

Meeting goes as planned, all questions are fielded and batted. Off they go with a smile on their face, job done! Glancing around, the second parent is nowhere to be seen. You know they are here because their delightful child has been running through the hall for the last forty minutes, screaming at the top of their lungs and crashing into everyone whilst riding the trike from reception. How did that get from KS1 to KS2 hall anyway? Four minutes have gone by. Perhaps they've thought better of it and gone home? That coffee break is creeping up fast. Maybe someone has even left chocolate biscuits in the staffroom. Oh, the joy, a coffee and a biscuit.

Six minutes late and with an armful of children, but no apology, the long awaited, much dreaded parent arrives. They sit down and slowly release their clan of children to wreak havoc on the tranquillity of the hall. Upon enquiry you are informed they are late because the last teacher in KS-1 over-ran and it took ages to get from one hall to the next. Glad to know parents took heed of the note about not booking back-to-back meetings if they have two or more siblings. Further enquiry reveals they haven't looked at their child's books as they can't understand their writing and their little bundle of joy hates math anyway.

This brings you round to the first point, attendance. While carefully and diplomatically dancing around the fact that said child has missed a large part of the term so far, you are interrupted by a random sibling with Lego wedged up its nose and crying for Mum's attention. You move on to writing style and attention span, while looking at your sign-up sheet and realising that Mum added her own name to the list, mis-spelling her surname. That answers the literacy-based element of your comment. Finally, you look at previous and predicted levels. Both well below the current year group, both well below national average and reasonable rate of acceleration.

Mum shrugs, it's all the schools fault anyway and then the bombshell that said child doesn't really like you as they feel you don't like them. One of these comments ring true. You slog on and make the best of a bad situation. You find positives in the child's natural love of PE and games, but not team sport or sharing, and you praise their growing love of arts and crafts. The meeting ends and your coffee break calls. Sadly, so does the next parent on the list as not only have you gone over time with Miss 'Six-Minutes Late', but you've also run over your allocated phantom parent. Fantastic! Will this night never end?!

Eventually it's 6.45 p.m. and the last parent has gone. Your coffee is cold, your body is tired, and you're the last member of staff in the hall besides the caretaker who is not looking pleased with you. You gather your things and return unseen trays of books back to the classroom, only to pick up thirty or more books which all need marking and feedback for tomorrow's parents evening.

Parents evening will not go away. They are here to stay and an essential part of the academic year. This being the case, embrace the madness. Know it's going to be a long two days. Accept that some parents will show, some wont, and some will take their allocated ten minutes and stretch it out for another ten. For every three or four parents who make your blood boil, you'll meet that one who is glad you cared. The one who's child it is a pleasure to teach, who's child stretches your knowledge and never your patience. That parent, that one there, will be the reason you smile, the reason you care and ultimately the reason you do what you do. Better than that? They will know all of this and thank you for it. And, when all is said and done, you can't ask for more. Well of course, more grateful and considerate parents. We can but dream.

Report Writing

This is your chance to tell the parents how well their child is doing

Once again as I reflect on my own childhood, I don't recall my school report being as detailed as they are today. I recall being asked to take home a single brown envelope with my parents' name on the front and wondering if I'd get a peek at the card without my parents knowing before I got home. I never did. My reports consisted of four columns: Subject, grade, comment, and teacher signature. It was a single sheet of paper full of illegible handwriting in various colours and always had a head teacher comment at the bottom. Mine always seemed to end with, 'Unless you want to become a comedian, I suggest you take next year much more seriously than you did this year, or you will have little to no future'. Well, I became a teacher, so what does that say about anything written in those reports?

Today the reports that come home are like mini biographies, prepared so meticulously they are like pieces of art.

To write a report, you need to have a deep insight into the child. This is obvious, as a teacher you need to comment on: What are they like academically, how are they performing compared to last year, what are their predicted assessment levels (If this data is not already included), or how did they perform against their predicted levels? To add to this, you need to comment on how they interact with both adults and their peers, what their strengths are, and what areas, if any, do they need to improve on moving forward. I've been to job interviews where less information is required!

All of the above information doesn't seem unreasonable. Especially if you're a parent, right? This is information you want and need to understand how your child is doing at school, and how they compare their peers.

From the teacher's perspective, writing reports is up there on the list of things I hated doing. My own personal experiences taught me the best way was not to procrastinate about what to write, and then write it two days before the submission date! I think this cycle happened every year, I never learnt!

From an outsider's point of view, it's hard to imagine why writing a report is so difficult. Again, a parent wouldn't understand what all the fuss is about. After all, a good teacher knows each and every one of their children, right? To a point, that statement is correct.

As a teacher, there are usually two types of children that stand out when it comes to report writing time. I referred to them as the 'ooos' and the 'ughs'. The former being the bright, well behaved, eager learners, with the latter being the exact opposite. I always found myself having enough material to write good, detailed reports about these children. Inevitably the 'ughs' were left until last, as they were the most depressing to write about. Merely jaded reminders of your own failures and their lack of willingness to engage for the whole year. The 'ooos' on the other hand, nothing but sheer joy to write about. Ego-boosting notes about how well they have done under your exceptional guidance, well planned, well resourced, engaging lessons.

This being said, what about the majority children? You know, the vanilla crowd. The larger part of the class who are not so outstanding, but just hovering at expected levels. The children who pottered along nicely, still needed intervention at times, but only to see them along, keep them on the straight and narrow. These children were the hardest to write about. Not quite hovering above the parapet to be classed as higher achievers, but also not so far behind they were always one-to-one intervention children. They contributed enough to make a lesson observation interesting. Ensuring 'stretch and challenge' was always addressed, but never quite hit the nail on the head when it really mattered. The mid-level group, the nice, friendly, smile and get on with it kids, who through no fault of their own, just faded into the background among their more rowdy, needy, and nerdy peers. These were the children that challenged the report writer more than any. If only you could write what you truly felt!

In most schools' report writing is a standard template, created by some over-zealous SLT member or downloaded from a local outstanding schools website. You'd think being a professional who has trained for three years, practiced for more than that and having specialised in English language, you'd have free reign to create and write your own class reports. Wrong! Each report must be read, sometimes by a colleague, usually by a member of SLT and / or the head. This means a submission date is given a week or two before the reports go out to parents. And teachers are asked to submit a higher-ability, mid-ability, and lower-ability example report. Obviously, these are the first three you write, and will no doubt be the templates for these groups. Moving forward, this is at least the plan.

Once the reports have been proof-read, the instruction on how to write all further reports follows: Specific font and size, banned phrases, the percentage of positive to negative comments, how much emphasis to place on academic progress over attendance and behaviour. If attendance and behaviour are an issue, be sure to mention this in a positive way and try to avoid this being the reason the child may not have made expected progress. The list goes on and then, before the all clear to proceed, you get the killer instruction: Please avoid, in all cases, using copy and paste to rewrite comments on reports. Specifically, those of you with siblings in your class. Dammit! Copy and past, the last saviour of the report.

So, the task of writing begins. Font style and size chosen, text box fixed to not expand, word limit per subject set, not forgetting of course the whole report must not exceed two pages, including head teacher comments. You begin with the 'ooos' as these are nice and easy to write, and words just flow from your fingers. Until you realise you have used a stock phrase in three reports. Amendments made, drafts rewritten, you've done your first six. Averaging about one to two hours per report. That's enough for one evening.

The following evening you write the 'ughs'. They are- easier to write than the vanilla bunch; and the perfect opportunity to unwind and unleash a year's worth of frustration. This is harder than you would imagine. How, for example, do you tactfully relay to a parent that their child has failed to improve their spelling due to lack of support at home? How do you respectfully tell a parent their child has failed to reach expected progress due to being absent a third of the term? In some scenarios, how do you inform a parent that their child's writing has passed through the eyes of several members of staff and is still illegible, despite a years' worth of 1-2-1 intervention? Once again, you rewrite repeated phrases from one report to the next and find you've spent more than two hours per report. And there are still several books to be marked.

Finally, your challenge, the mid-level, vanilla bunch. No repetition of stock phrases, lack of any real inspiration for the lovely, likeable but hard to progress group causes immediate writer's block. How to tackle this? Split the group into the ones who have made progress and the ones who have not. Start with the former, pulling out evidential examples dating back to term 1 and commenting on their willingness to progress and eagerness to always partake in group discussion. Next, the latter. The group who has made minimal progress despite all intervention. The group who just tip into mid-ability, the loveable, perennial triers who neither struggle nor inspire. Painstaking hours, writing and rewriting comments. Justifying the minimal progress without your teaching being called into question. Deciding what to include and what to omit. Hours spent producing well worded, well-structured reports. Your only wish? That each parent spends the time reading them.

Once written, all reports are then sent to the head to add their valuable yearly comments for children they have mostly become accustomed to passing in corridors, telling off in assemblies, or giving out weekly awards to. At best, your reports will be returned with missing punctuation errors and the occasional sentence reworded. At worse, the head teacher does not like the tone of your comment or feels more positives can be added. Depending on your year group, these reports will be returned in good time, or with two days to submission and delivery. My experience has been that year two and six reports get priority, then EYFS, and finally years 3-5. So, heaven help the year 4 teacher whose tone is not favoured, as you have exactly two days to rewrite and re-submit your many hours' worth of effort.

It always amused me to get my reports finalised and read the headteacher's comments. After weeks of being reminded not to duplicate stock phrases, before my very eyes, exactly that. A clear lack of any personal knowledge, understanding of progress, and generally who each child was, all summed up in two sentences. Each ending with, 'I wish you all the best for journey into next year'. (Thanks for that, great input, you're really earning your £55,000 salary!).

The general feeling was a small percentage of parents would actually read the reports, and a smaller percentage would read them with their children. So, after hours, days and weeks of perfecting and refining comments at the detriment of your sleep, social life and marking, you are secure in the knowledge most children won't have a clue what you wrote in their report and most parents will never question your comments. All except that single example in which you refer to 'him' as 'her' or called 'David' 'Joanne', typical!

Just like most elements of the job, report writing is now as essential as registration at 9 a.m. It's always going to need doing, will never be easy, or come at a welcome time. My advice is to take the best of the bunch and leave them until last. End on a high. Get them all written and reflect on what a great job you've done in getting them finished. Finally, re-read those pieces of art which were a sheer joy to compose.

Reading them back will make you realise it's not all doom and gloom and that you, the class teacher, are having an impact on some of the children in your class. These will be the children whose parents will read and absorb every word in each one of those boxes on the report pro forma.

These are the parents who will stop you in the following days and give a little thank-you. That thank-you will mean the world to you.

Behaviour Management

Remember, the way your class behave is a direct reflection on you and the school

I am the first person to admit-that at school I was no angel. I am sure the likes of Mr. Dear (Math), Mr. Lever (English), Mrs. McDonald (Head teacher), Mr. & Mrs. Hawes (Psycho husband and wife math and French teachers), and Mr. Benn (Head teacher) will all clarify this in abundance. I disliked each and every one of them. At the time, school was more like a social club to me. A place to meet up with your friends, meet girls, get into fights, and occasionally learn something. I wasn't academic, often fighting against learning, and those who wanted to help me learn. I just didn't see the point. I didn't have aspirations until much later in school and, as such, found school and learning pointless. This being said, I did manage to achieve in some areas when I applied myself. Math bored me; however, English really ignited my interests. Specifically writing. I always flourished when it came to story writing or storytelling. I was a show-off at school and loved attention, so being given the opportunity to stand up and read out from a book or share a story is where I would really shine. I excelled in the less obvious areas of the curriculum. Home economics or cookery, as it was known then. Not your traditional route for a GCSE option, but I took it. I loved to cook, make, and bake things I could take home and share with my family. History was another area I enjoyed. CDT, art, and music were all subjects I took. But I was never very patient and couldn't be bothered with waiting to create things. I always wanted instant gratification. My talent in woodwork extended not far beyond rubbing metal files together to create sparks, gluing anything and everything together with a hot glue gun, and smacking nails in to the workbench. Although I do recall making a very nice, cow shaped newspaper rack which I still have to this day.

Considering my own attitude to learning it was a miracle I was never given the cane. Although, it has to be recognised that by time my own behaviour was at its worse, the cane had long been abolished. And boy was my backside grateful for that! There were times when my school days saw little actual learning and more of the inside of a head teachers office than I care to remember. Being in class was hard. I always had something to say and, regardless of whether it was right or wrong, relevant or not, I shouted it out. Or made stupid noises with my arm raised and hand waving in the air!

The thing is, in each class I always knew my limits. I knew how far I could push each teacher before they would get to the point of kicking me out and sending me to another class, or the head. Mostly the stare would do it, the teacher glare, the killer eyes, call it whatever, that usually worked. When I was at school it was not uncommon for a teacher to blow their top and hurl a piece of chalk at me, throw a board rubber to the floor in anger, or even wrap my knuckles with a wooden ruler for not holding my pencil correctly. Teachers would call my parents, demand they come to the school, and take me home. Headteachers would call my parents in for minor infringements and make me stand and explain my behaviour, before then agreeing that home was the best place for me. For the meantime at least.

Me getting kicked out of class was either because my behaviour in previous years or preceding classes had been so bad that my reputation proceeded me. And I was actually out the class before I even stepped a foot in it. If that wasn't the reason, it was because I had an older brother who also had a similar approach to his learning and attitude towards school. The teacher automatically assumed this was hereditary and moved me to another class on surname alone. My behaviour choices were my own and, at the time, seemed either funny or just part of the journey through education. I was suspended once. I was caught fighting twice in the same week and the school had really had enough and decided I was to be punished with a week at home. My parents were so angry that after just two days I was praying for some chalk to be thrown at me, or even a ruler to strike me over the knuckles. As school progressed and I got older (Note, not matured) I realised the only thing holding back a fantastic school experience was me. I never aspired to be a clown, so I decided I should stop acting like one and perhaps knuckle down. I made good ground, too, surprising both teachers and classmates with what I could achieve when I wanted to. Reports got better, learning became more enjoyable, and school became a place I enjoyed rather than rejected. All the time I knew one slip and that stare, raised voice, or flying piece of pink chalk would hit me and knock me back.

Reflectively, I apologise to every teacher who ever tried. To the teachers who cared for me and my learning. To those teachers who always turned the other cheek or just wanted the best for me and persisted with me. I'm sorry. I'm sorry I was 'that child'. I'm sorry I tested you. I'm sorry I underappreciated your value and your wisdom.

In schools today, behaviour management is something very different to what I experienced in class when I was younger. In fact, behaviour management warrants its own degree course given the amount of different sanctions and rewards that exist in schools today. The teaching degree will not teach you how to manage behaviour, behaviour types, and children who want to fight the world and you!

School's behaviour policies may dress themselves up in many guises but trust me they are all the same. Whether it be an unhappy face drawn on the board, a sliding scales of happy / sad faces, hot air balloons rising for success and sinking lower for unacceptable behaviour or notches on a number chart, they all amount to the same course of action. What is that course of action? Usually: A verbal warning (I know what you're doing). A second verbal warning / yellow card (I still know what you're doing and am now slightly annoyed). Final yellow card (now you are really pissing me off!) then moving the child from their desk to another area of the classroom, so ultimately they can go misbehave on another table. And finally, the red card. Moving them to another class and removing some sort of reward (Usually minutes from their golden time). So, remember that's three opportunities to misbehave before they are sent to another class, out of your hair… to misbehave in that class, too. Providing that class teacher with an opportunity to question your actions and choices.

Any teacher, teaching today or who has taught in the last ten years or more will tell you that one of the most exhausting parts of their day is not the marking, not the planning, and not the teaching. It's the management of those special little angels who all come with different behavioural issues and all require different interventions to help them just sit, listen, and learn. Very few of which you will be taught about on your degree course. Today a smack round the head is no longer classed as a suitable intervention – sadly!

It is true every child deserves to be rewarded and recognised for one thing, something they do that really stands out above and beyond and I couldn't agree more. There are hundreds of children in schools who achieve greatness on a daily basis but go unrecognised. Children producing the most amazing written work, writing stories far above and beyond anyone's expectations. Children working towards and achieving mastery level in Math, solving, and explaining Math's problems two years above their current year group. There are children with creativity in abundance, excelling in music, art, and design who remain unappreciated and unacknowledged for the large part of their school life. Why is this happening? Because the largest part of the teacher's day is taken up with managing the smaller parts of their class, the minority who have what is labelled as 'behavioural issues'.

Children today walk into your class with a whole plethora of behaviour issues and you, as the teacher, are expected to be able to deal with and plan for every single one of them. Part of your training is how to deal with bad, or unacceptable behaviour. The theory behind this is relatively simple in its delivery and as such, you will always have ringing in your ears the voices of your university tutors, 'You are the adult in the situation, and you will deal with misbehaviour in line with the schools behaviour policy'. (I failed many times).

'You must also remember that, as the professional in the scenario, taking charge does not mean you will belittle, embarrass, or make the child feel inferior to his or her peers'. (Once again, I failed many times). You must also never forget, 'Behind every action that falls outside of the behaviour policy, there is a reason, or many reasons, for the child's behaviour and you must think about these reasons before applying any sanction which could make the situation worse'. The reason usually being lazy parents, too busy for their own child!

At the start of any new academic year, you will be handed over from the previous class teacher or school many, many folders. All of which you will need to read and absorb before any child walks into your class. These will include previous and current assessment results, medical issues, details of special dietary requirements, and behaviour issues. The behaviour folder is usually the largest folder. As you read through this you will take note of specific names and challenging behaviours each of these names demonstrate. To add to this, you will note an ongoing behaviour management records containing a list of tried and tested methods which have all been used to try and engage those specific individuals. As you plough your way through, you will read about failed behaviour interventions, specific targeted behaviour plans, and tailored meetings led by outside behaviour support groups. All of which have failed, or not been supported in one way or another. Meanwhile, the words of your university tutors are still rattling around your head, 'Every child deserves a chance. Every child has good inside them. You can turn all behaviours around with the right lesson and the right resources'. All you can think is, 'Why me?'

Contained in the folder dating back to reception years or even records from another school, you will find learning support workers reports. Reports written by observers, who have tried to find root causes of the behaviours and even tried to justify it, so it blends into the child's school experience. Paper trails worthy of small forests are written about the child. Their family history, the many fathers they have had, the plights of mother's own school experiences, and the many tests they have encountered for ADHD, dyslexia, dyspraxia, boredom, even disliking male teachers. All of which have resulted in the same outcome: Not known or present. So, for all your reading you discover you have one or more 'naughty' child in your class who blames everyone for their behaviour, except themselves.

Once the teacher has understood all of this, they need to decide which sanction to apply. In normal circumstances the behaviour being displayed would be straight to red card, do not pass go, do not collect £200. This, however, is not 'normal' because this is one of those particular children who dodges the class behaviour system because they have their very own tailored behaviour support plan. A plan written specifically for them based on historic behaviours, medication, learning styles, and every other excuse the parents have used to ensure their child gets that little bit of extra tolerance from everyone they happen to collide with.

Children with behaviour issues (In my day, these children would just have been called 'naughty children' or far worse) seem all too aware of what 'issues' they have. Therefore, arming them with the knowledge that their behaviours, chosen or not, can be excused ('because mum told me it's not my fault!'). It seems to be an all too familiar concept today for children to be labelled, rightly or wrongly, and the parents and children use that label to seek extra loopholes in the system and use them as excuses.

Many was the time I would have children tell *me* what was wrong with *them* and then this be used to try an excuse behaviours. 'I'm sorry I threw my chair, Sir, I have anger issues' or 'I can't do this work, Sir, because I can't concentrate long enough as I have attention disorder'. Even, 'Sir, if you don't let me go to the toilet, I'm going to kick off because you know I have anger rages'. My conclusion from this is that parent's arm- their children with information so that they can shift the blame to the teacher and / or the school when their little angels play up.

Parents are seeking reasons for the unacceptable behaviours and will always start at school, never at home. Too add to this, it seems if parents push hard enough, the schools will seek medical assessments and behaviour managements specialist all in the name of labelling a child. Once the label is attached, who does it fall to manage the child? The parents? The local authority? No. The teacher. The teacher who has twenty-eight other children to teach, engage, manage, and to nurture.

There is little wonder that behaviour management is one of the biggest challenges in school today. There are too many systems in place, too many reports to read, and too many behaviour plans to try and juggle. What works for the majority does not work for the minority and it is the minority that will cause the lion's share of behaviour related issues in class. Schools today seem reluctant to implement detention, loss of break times, or periods of suspension because each one of these options involves too much paperwork and intervention. I have seen children run teachers, teaching assistants, and lunchtime supervisors ragged in the pursuit of misbehaving. Children can seemingly start wars with particular adults, if they have a behaviour plan and the sanctions very rarely outweigh the carnage. These children don't conform to, or even care about, school behaviour procedures. They come to school with one thing in mind, to see how far they can push their teachers, their peers, and everyone around them. And in the end, the only people who lose out are those children who come in- with the sole aim of learning, moving on, and achieving their best.

As a male teacher in a primary school setting, you are usually the minority. Being the minority, as a teacher, will usually mean taking a different approach to things. Be it behaviour management, music lessons, PE, or playground duty. You want to stand out for being more than just a male in school. In my case, it was behaviour management. I always set my expectations high and rewarded those who met them. I made it my aim early September to ensure my children knew I did not come to school to shout. I respected my children as they respected me and shared things with them beyond the class. My favourite foods, my dog's name, what I did before teaching, and tastes in music.

Things like this seemed to gain me respect and, as such, the children wanted to behave. Did I ever encounter misbehaviour? Of course, I did in large amounts some years. Did these children challenge me? Yes, every day for most of the year. Did I crack and let them get to me? Of course, I am only human. There were times I forgot about being the adult in the scenario. Times I wished I hadn't engaged in argumentative conversations with them. It's hard to 'be the adult' when a child swears at you, throws their books to the floor, storms out of class and hits their own head against a wall, to later claim it was you who had struck them. Before all of this, I always tried my best to understand, to help, and to seek answers as to why. I didn't always find them. Overall, I would say I had some of my best achievements turning some of these children around. Not totally, this would require 1-2-1 intervention for the whole academic year.

For me, the challenge of turning around attitudes, behaviours, and responses to learning were some of my proudest moments. Maybe I understood some of these children. Maybe, looking back on my own experiences at school, I could relate to them. While I accept my own school experiences were not the greatest, I do not accept that I played the system the way some do today. I do understand school is not easy for all, that one behaviour shoe does not fit the masses. I also accept that everyone has the right to be treated equally and fairly while they are in the teacher's care. I always accepted these points and maybe that's why behaviour was less of an issue for me than it was for previous or future teachers. That being said, when I did face behaviour related issues, they were big, challenging, and consumed my day. I often forgot the voices of my tutors and did my own thing. Not by the book, not considering the school policy, but it worked.

Behaviour in schools will always be a concern, to governors, headteachers, teachers, and statisticians. In my experience, teachers who encounter little to no behaviour challenges are few and far between and are indeed the lucky few. Given the influences on children today, T.V, social media, computer gaming, and larger families, then poor behaviour isn't going to just go-away. A teacher can only hope to curtail bad behaviour choices or manage sociably acceptable behaviour in their class. There is no secret to doing this. Be firm, be fair. Be bold in your choices and stick to your decisions, right, wrong, or indifferent. Make sure you follow through on sanctions, don't make empty threats. Children will manipulate empty threats and carry on, regardless of what you say. Children respect firm and fair teachers. Children will always push the boundaries, but the teacher will always move those boundaries just at the right time, so the child never gets the upper hand. If you manage to maintain acceptable-behaviour for all, then this should be seen as a daily win.

School Trips

Enjoy your day, don't lose any children and remember the first-aid kit

On reflection back to my own childhood, school trips were really quite non-eventful. I recall a trip to the local museum, Alton Towers theme park (I fail to make the educational link in that one!) and a foreign exchange trip to Paris, which I didn't take part in. Beyond this, my memory doesn't recall many experiences of venturing beyond the school gates. This is not to say school trips did not happen, I am sure they did. My memory fails to recall any memorable experiences, involving a school trip, which shaped me as a learner or as an adult.

As a teacher, the school trip is as far away from the day out / Jolly you expect it to be, and often is more stressful than a day in the class. While parents see it as an excuse to get out of class, the reality is it's a day spend counting, screaming, form filling, and… counting.

At the start of the term, when all of your topic plans are submitted, it is favourable if you can also build into those plans any suggestions you have for a field trip / topic-based school trip. While this may sound easy enough, this is September and you are having to submit ideas for a proposed trip in January, April or even July. This is the first (Inset) day of the term and you're being asked, 'Where are you planning to go for your school trip in November or March?'

The reality is, you've only just planned your first day back, so your school trip is way down the ever-growing to-do list.

In some schools I've worked in, the yearly class trip(s) are set in stone, along with the topics, and these are the trips you are expected to arrange. Regardless of your input as the teacher, regardless of relevance, they are firmly in place, and you will work them into your yearly plan. So, you will be teaching the Romans as a topic, and you will be expected to go to an amphitheatre as part of that topic. Children have been studying the Romans for years at this school and as such, children expect to be taken to the amphitheatre, it's become a year 4 tradition!

At these schools you plan the trip, but you don't decide the location, or the time of year. No, in these schools you follow the plans from previous years, and these plans dictate your trip. In these schools the cost of the trip is usually decided, the coach company expects the call to confirm the booking, and the risk assessment is already done (just change the date, the names of the teachers, and add the names of the vulnerable children in the appropriate column).

While it may seem like an easier gig with the location, date, and assessments already decided, it does leave very little flexibility or manoeuvre for excitement within the topic. From a teaching perspective, these types of trips rarely serve any purpose and need to be shoe-horned into the topic to make the upcoming day out remotely relevant. You spend hours planning lessons based around the amphitheatre. Where were they? What where they? What happened there? What significance did they make to the era? What will we do when we get there? Why are we going? Who even cares? Shall we bother at all? Is there a gift shop? Will we need a change of clothes? Enough questions to make you want to scream, while your head explodes at the very thought of the whole day. Of course, it could be worse. You could be teaching *'Local landscapes and areas of interest'* and preparing to take your children to a local beach to discuss rock formation, cliff erosion, and how sand is formed (yes, I did that one and a thrilling day it was too!).

In summary, where a pre-planned trip is already decided for you, you end up feeling like a spare part, a small cog in a churning machine, struggling to understand why the trip even bears any relevance anymore. You fiddle with the paperwork, collect the money, and move the children through the system like the teacher who originally thought of the idea several years ago.

You do, of course, have the other extreme. The schools whose ambition doesn't match the affordability of the demographic and leaves all expectation on you to plan the best school trip the year group have ever seen. One which will be talked about for the rest of the school year.

In these schools the class trip must be justified in all aspects. As the teacher you have to justify the educational benefit to the head, the bursar, and the parents. To add to this, you have to decide the location, time of year, book the coach, write the letter, collect the permission slips, and justify why the parents should contribute to the cost. 'Coaches don't pay for themselves' and 'Attractions won't let us in for free' are two of the responses which are unacceptable! In addition to this, there is the dreaded risk-assessment. A lousy, pointless, bureaucratic lead bit of red-tape which every teacher must complete for any event taking place outside of the classroom.

Nothing, and I do mean nothing, can take place without this twenty-four-page document being completed.

And so, at the very start of term, it begins. You skim the topics you have been allocated or inherited for the year, and desperately look at where you can shoe-horn a trip into the already busy school year. In your own head, you want it to be in the summer term. Why? The weather will be better, the children won't have exams to worry about (Depending on your year group), and more importantly, you can use the trip as a carrot for the whole year to promote good behaviour. And a bribe to the perennial misbehaver who comes with more baggage that several 747s departing to Ibiza! However, you soon find out a trip during summer term won't happen, as that slot has already been booked and agreed by another year group. This leaves you with a trip in the first term or early in the New Year, neither option is ideal. Again, referring to your topic plan, your heart sinks as you see neither topic for these times promote excitement or any ounce of joy in your now heavy heart. At best, in a two-form entry school, you have a partner teacher who is somewhat more excited than you and they make the location suggestion. At worse, you're in a one form entry school and you have no idea where to plan a school trip linked to *'Growing and developing'* or *'The Rainforest and their destruction'*.

Eventually, you will make a decision. Be it you're forced into one or you look back at previous trips, discuss options with other teachers or you are directed by the power of Google: 'Location close to me... Rainforest...year 5...UK'. This will then become cemented into the yearly planner and is where the work begins.

Prior to the actual day, the list of jobs the teacher has to do in preparation for the actual trip is endless. While in no particular order, let me take you through the pre-trip checklist.

1 – The educational purpose of the trip:

What will the children get from going on the trip? A hint, 'Their only trip out for the whole year' is not an acceptable answer. Neither is, 'An opportunity to see life beyond their estate'. My recommendation would be to avoid these responses and look to find the more suitable, politically correct answers. As hard as it may seem, there has to be a reason the trip is justified, and educational link, no matter how tenuous, will swing the head's decision. So, make it count. You will need to find out if the proposed location has an education centre, a tour guide, or an activity area where children can be educationally creative and demonstrate anything they have learnt. Again, this is where Google comes into its own. The earlier the research is done, the more likely you can make a link to something in the curriculum or within your plans. When all else fails, make up the educational purpose and wait to be challenged!

2 – Informing the parents:

When and how will the parents be informed? The teacher will need to inform the parents of the proposed trip. This means you will need to practise your best diplomatic letter writing skills. Don't forget, no correspondence leaves the school without the head's approval. You could use the school online portal to inform all parents, but this does depend on them taking the time to log in, acknowledge and tick the permission box, as well as send an online payment. To add to this, you can't expect all parents to have online access, can you?

A letter it is. Your letter will need to include: Where you intend to go, what time of year will it be, what time will the children leave school, and be back, what clothes they will need, (Coats, wellingtons, sensible shoes, gloves, waterproof jackets, etc), what type of food is acceptable and not acceptable, what food is provided for free school meal children, how much money, if any, each child can take, and a list of adults who will accompany the children on the trip. Finally, the cost. The dreaded request for money to fund the trip. The audacity you show asking each parent for £9.99 to cover a coach, entry fee, and educational tour included in the trip. This needs to be bold, clear, and worded well as the number of payments will decide if the trip goes ahead or not.

In my day, if you wanted to go on a school trip you returned the permission slip inside an envelope with the associated fee requested. Easy, you pay, you went. If you didn't pay, you were sent to another class for the day while your class boarded the coach and left for Alton Towers. Today is very different. You, as the teacher, have to consider the amount of money you ask for. Is it reasonable to ask each parent for £9.99? Can the trip and the associated activities be justified? Can the single parent afford the £9.99? I mean, these are the parents with the perfect hair extensions, the latest iPhones hanging out their jeans, and the perfectly manicured false nails. Is it right to be asking them for money to send one of their four children on a trip? What if mum and / or dad can't afford it? Does that mean their child won't go? Will that child be singled out, left at school missing the trip? To add to this, if two or three parents don't pay then why should the other twenty-seven? How will you handle that? So now your role as teacher has become event planner, financial advisor, and United Nations peace negotiator. You didn't expect this when you planned this trip, did you?

3 – Booking the coach:

An easy enough job, right? Call the local coach depot, as recommended by the school secretary, confirm the date, time, and number of children, wallop! Coach booked.

No, this would be far too simple. Firstly, the coach company wants confirmation of where they are going. This needs to be sent in an e-mail. Next, how long will the driver be out? All day, or can he go off and come back? Have you considered which is the quickest route, or is there a preferred route? I mean, really? You're the teacher not the bus driver, how do you know?! You'll also need to provide specific parking details for outside the school and the venue if you don't want your class walking ten minutes to and from the coach because access was tricky at this time of day.

Usually, the coach company wants a deposit, this must be paid before the trip and will secure the coach. This means speaking nicely to the secretary and asking her to release funds in lieu of any payments coming in for the actual trip. Made even harder by the fact you only have two permission slips returned and one of those is free school meals!

With the deposit paid and times confirmed, the coach company then tells you they only have one bus free for the required time slot, and their company policy is one adult per ten children. Meaning you require three adults minimum. Luckily, the school policy is one adult per nine children, so you have one adult spare. With all obstacles negotiated, the coach is booked, and all you require is a confirmation e-mail. You are told this will follow, so onwards and upwards.

4 – The risk assessment*:

A risk assessment: The method of identifying any potential risk factors or hazards that have the potential to cause harm or distress. An evaluation of any risk that could occur and be deemed hazardous.

Prior to the trip, any child leaving the school grounds as part of the school day or any thought that you, an actual trusted professional, will accompany anyone out in the big, wide world, you must complete a risk assessment. This, you will find out, is a local authority requirement and will become the basis of which you are able to responsibly plan and carry-out a school trip.

In most schools I taught in, the risk assessment involved looking back at last year's trip, downloading that year's risk assessment to your T-drive and changing dates and names to match those of your class. This was not standard practise. In two schools it was procedure to attend site in your own time, walk through the day, and identify risks and hazards which you felt could impact on the proposed day. I did this twice. On one occasion I failed to identify that a trip to the local zoo where children could feed goats could actually involve a child losing a finger or becoming infected by rancid animals. Despite the fact we would NOT be doing this. On the other occasion, I failed to observe the proposed hazard that a child could drown in the sea while at the beach. Despite the fact I had observed the tide would be out at the proposed time of the visit. What can I say? I missed the module on risk assessments at university.

While I appreciate the value of the risk assessment, in my experience, they are completed not for the safety of the teacher and protection of the children. More to be placed in a folder so they can be produced in the event the local authority or Ofsted inspectors should happen to drop-in unexpectedly. Teachers would be less inclined to see these assessments as a chore if there was actual uniformity across schools or local authorities.

Of course, I understand the importance of correctly completing a risk assessment. They are there to protect everyone and make sure the day goes ahead without any accident or incident. No teacher wants any school trip to result in any child under their supervision being hurt or harmed. A well-researched and thorough risk assessment will identify any hazards and ensure a risk-free day for all attending. And no child will be losing their fingers to rancid goats or drowning in the sea. No matter how far the tide may be out, or how much you wish they would.

5 – Ordering food:

As a class teacher, each day starts with registration, the point of the day where you identify who eats school meals, who has a packed lunch, and who does and does not pay for their meals. A school trip is no different, right? Not so much, as you would expect. The standard procedure for a school trip is that everyone will bring a suitable packed lunch. Those children who are FSM will be provided with one by the school. If you remember to order them from the school kitchen two to three weeks in advance that is.

You cannot guarantee the proposed location will have facilities or provide lunch. Packed lunch covers off all areas of who eats what and who likes what... or so you'd think. More often than not, most children will bring a packed lunch deemed suitable by the school. Suitable is usually a sandwich, bag of crisps, piece of fruit, and a non-chocolate-based snack. There are, however, those children who will bring a packed lunch which will feed not only the child themselves, but their entire class, parent helpers, teaching assistants, and any other visitors to the attraction on that day. Easy to identify, these children bring a rucksack on the day, specifically given to house the oversized packed lunch container of choice. While you suspect this may be the case, you ignore it at the start of the day, and only have your suspicions confirmed at the designated lunch stop some four hours later.

As you seat the class for lunch, your carefully placed cup of tea begins to ripple, somewhat reminiscent of the scene in *Jurassic Park*. You look around and see that one child, the one you suspected would be the one, hauling out of their rucksack the largest food container you have ever seen. The table positively buckles under the weight of their lunchtime load. A quick walk of the room and you notice a container filled with: Billy Bear Ham, cheese strings, Monster munch crisps, a pork pie, sausage rolls, and ketchup sachets. All is not lost though, they have bananas... chocolate covered ones from the pick and mix counter! Note to self, speak with mum after school. Second note to self, isn't that family FSM? Didn't they only pay half of the required £9.99 trip fee? Is this the child who gets out of breath tying their shoelaces? Finally, to add to this, you observe the other FSM children who have only eaten the crisps element of their school provided lunch.

On enquiry you find out, 'I don't like white bread' or 'I don't eat cheese and ham in the same sandwich'. They say beggars can't be choosers, right? Final note to self, expect these children's parent to complain that their child went hungry all day. Your lunch, on the other hand, consisted of a now cold cup of tea, half spilt by the appearance of the *Jurassic Park* lunch, and a warm, wilted sandwich you left out on the table pre-dinner hall walk through.

6- The first aid kit:

No school trip is complete, or even considered, without someone taking responsibility for the first aid kit. Granted, you are not first aid trained, you have zero medical training and, more importantly, there are no children in your class with allergies. But nevertheless, you must have a fully stocked first aid kit attached and clipped to someone's belt on the day. Usually, yours! You'll carry it around all day, full of blue plasters, inhalers, and anti-bacterial wipes. Every child on the trip will remind you not to forget it. Your parent helpers and teaching assistants will join in the chorus of screams, constantly reminding you not to leave it on the bus, table, or chair for the whole of the day. And, as the end of the day arrives, not one single person, child or adult, has needed any form of medical attention. Leave it at school, or on the bus and you'll soon be inundated with cut fingers, bruises, cuts, and grazes. Not forgetting a random asthma attack!

7 – The reflective jackets:

Nothing says school trip like the good old fluorescent / high visibility jacket! More important than any factor of the actual day is the reflective jacket. Like moths to the flame, children will scoop up their jackets. They have gone all the way through school knowing that the school trip equates to the ill-fitting, high visibility jacket. You'll search high and low for these, and eventually find them in the PE cupboard or under the stage. Smelling slightly mouldy from the last time they were used and returned wet from the sudden downpour which dampened the previous school trip. Every school will have them. Every school will have just one box. The box will contain a class set of jackets, and all in various states of worn and torn. Usually, one short of an actual full class set, and too small or too large for your class.

All that said, every child must wear one for the whole day, because you happened to tick the box on the risk assessment. Moving around like a firefly, you'll be counting these jackets all day. Once on the children, off the children, left on the bus, and various rest stops. At the end of the trip, you'll return them nicely folded and counted to the box from which you took them from six hours earlier.

The best any teacher can hope for is: The day goes ahead without any incident, the children enjoy the day, each one of them having had an appropriate packed lunch, the coach turned up, both ends of the trip, on time, and no child suffered from travel sickness. As all teachers know, this is the dream day and very often it remains that way… a dream.

The school trip is a minefield and has the capacity to be the worst thing you decided to do out of the whole academic year. The list of potential disasters that can occur on the day is both endless and out of your control. You'll spend weeks worrying about the arrival of the bus, the attendance on the day, travel sickness, children eating on the bus, someone forgetting their bag / high visibility vest / packed lunch, and all of these things come second to the weather o the day. Typically, if you plan an indoor event, it will be too hot, and children will overheat. Which will make removal of high visibility vest imminent upon arrival. Or you plan an outdoor event and it's the wettest day on record, and no one remembered their sensible shoes or raincoat. Thus, you become the worst teacher to exist for planning such an ill-timed event on that given day.

There are the days when someone, somewhere is smiling down on you and your school trip is the best planned event scheduled that year. The children are full of excitement for a genuine fun day out. The bus turns up with a happy driver, a bus where all the seatbelts work, and the children sit together in sensibly chosen pairs. The sun is shining, but not so much it's uncomfortable. Arrival is swift and upon departure from the bus, children are checking each other to make sure they have their own bags and drinks bottles. The destination has prepared for the arrival of primary aged children and have appropriate numbers of staff to assist. The children all assemble for lunch, all present and correct, with 'school legal' packed lunches. You even manage a warm cup of tea and a sandwich, surrounded by smiling children, laughing at your sandwich of choice. The day goes to plan, and no injuries or incidents are recorded. Departure back to school is swift and comfortable, and you arrive back just as the end of day bell sounds.

To end a perfect day, parents are all waiting to collect their children on time, and no one has left a single item on the bus. Finally, you go back to school, return the class-set of jackets to the PE cupboard and leave, if you're lucky, before the rush hour traffic

Lesson Observations

*Our opportunity to see you deliver quality
first teaching*

As a child in school, I cannot recall being aware that my class teacher was being observed by other members of staff at the same time he or she was delivering a lesson to me. I've thought about this, and my memory cannot cast back to a time when I arrived in class, ready to start a lesson, and three other members of staff were perched on chairs, notebooks in hand, just waiting for the lesson to begin. Yes, there were times when other members of staff came into a lesson. Usually, the member of staff entering the room would refer to the class teacher by his or her first name, and the class would erupt into fits of giggles. These interruptions were mostly ad-hoc and rarely meant to disrupt the class.

As part of a teacher's professional development and depending on what stage they are at in their career, they will be observed either once a term or once every other term. The logic behind an observation is that members of the SLT (Senior leadership team) and / or the head see a teacher deliver a lesson, ensuring specific elements of the national curriculum, behaviour management, and classroom organisation are being adhered to. In addition to this, ensuring the lesson is delivered to a classroom of children who are engaged, intrigued, and taught appropriately at differing levels of ability. The observation will form part of a fair appraisal system which supports staff development, as well as improving pupil outcomes. Teachers are given the opportunity to receive meaningful and direct feedback about their practice and can also inform the development in any areas of improvement.

Prior to becoming a teacher, I worked in other sectors of industry. I started my working life training to be a car mechanic before going on to retail management, then finance, including pensions and mortgage advice. Not once, in any of these roles, do I recall my workmates, immediate line managers, or senior managers pulling up a chair, watching me work, and then going off to talk to the people I worked with about what they had just seen. Of course, there were appraisal meetings and performance reviews, these were usually target driven and done together with a dedicated line manager.

In teaching, the lesson observation will make or break you. It can break your confidence, your spirit, your purpose, and make you question your own understanding.

Ideally, before any lesson observation takes place, there will be an opportunity for the reviewer(s) and the teacher to meet at an agreed time to discuss the purpose and the focus of the observed lesson. This will usually include who the observers are, how long they will stay, and when you will all meet back post-observation to discuss findings. I read this somewhere... I don't recall where.

As with most things in this book, the lesson observation and the lead up to can vary from school to school, and there tends to be two ways these things are approached and carried out.

School number one, the worst-case scenario will usually take the following format: You walk into school one morning and you read on the staff notice board / termly calendar that lesson observations will commence this week. On some occasions you read who is carrying out the observations, in others you won't know. In black capital letters you may read what year group will be observed on which day or you may not.

So, armed with the minimal amount of information, you have a rough idea that your year group will be observed on Thursday. You don't know what time, who by, and which lesson. This now increases your workload by endless amounts. Will you be observed in numeracy or literacy? The school is having a big push on writing this term, but there were new incentives in numeracy on the last in-set day. You cover your options and decide it could be either. Of course, you already have Thursday's lessons planned. What you don't have is a lesson plan worthy of an observation, or any form of scrutiny from your head, senior team, or subject leaders. It's ok though, you can work with what you have. Unless it's coming towards the end of term, and you had an 'assessment lesson' or 'topic recap' lesson planned. In these cases, you need to start from scratch.

The lesson plan:

Despite thinking you have it in hand, you will find yourself rewriting your lesson plans, searching for more resources, and redeploying your teaching assistant. Probably several times over the next three hours of planning. You know in your head that if a one-hour lesson takes three hours to plan, you've overdone it and it's not worth the output. Despite this, you plough on regardless. You will look at every aspect of your lesson plan, and make sure there is no margin for error or misinterpretation. The learning objective will be clear, concise, and relevant to the previous days lesson and the following days session. You will have differentiated your plan five ways with clear objectives for each activity and making sure both you and your teaching assistant are working with a group each. Making sure you sit with the more challenging group and your teaching assistant sits with the more able group or is, at least, sat with the stretch and challenge group.

Each resource for each group offers a range of work and relevant resources, which shows current knowledge and understanding. As well as a suitable challenge that everyone in the group can achieve. In addition to all of this, you have included in each group activity an opportunity for the children to work independently and work as a group. So, their knowledge can be shared and demonstrated in written form and verbal reasoning. Now your group activities are sorted, and the adults have been suitably and realistically placed. You need just the right amount of teacher input for the opening and the plenary. You plan the lesson input to within an inch of perfection. Just enough talk to explain the learning objective, mixed questioning with a no hands-up Q&A session, before carefully explaining and leading into the main session.

Finally, your plenary. The point everything needs to wrap up and you need to demonstrate that every group achieved their objective, they understood what they did and why. The lesson plan shows a nice mix of assessment questions and evidence of work examples, ensuring teacher led groups have modelled what they achieved. There you have it, two beautifully scripted, colour-coded, assessment for learning based lesson plans (One for you and one for your T.A), ready for scrutiny and perfect delivery. All you need to do now is print multiple copies and leave them on empty chairs, ready for the observers…whoever that may be.

It would be remiss of me not to look at the other, nicer, and more realistic side of lesson observations and lesson planning. In these schools things are less time consuming.

School number two, the best, more ideal scenario: Lesson observations are planned well in advance. You are offered an AM or a PM timeslot, knowing if you decide upon an AM the following observation will be a PM. There is no panic about who will observe you because if you chose a 9 a.m. slot, you know that your timetable shows numeracy which means both the head and the numeracy subject lead will be observing you. SO, you know who, when, and what in terms of the subject. At times, you'll even know what the focus of the observation will be.

You look ahead at your lesson plan. You have followed the school's requirements and used the correct planning pro forma. The school asks you to highlight where the teaching assistant will be and what the learning objective will be. In terms of required elements this is all. It's clear from your plan who is getting adult support and the L.O is clear to see. In terms of lesson preparation, your resources, as indicated on the plan, are ready and you are confident that you're happy to be observed. This is the school observing you to help you develop professionally and to ensure you're adhering to the development plan. You email the lesson plan to your head and subject lead, and they have acknowledged its receipt.

School number one – the lesson:

In the worst-case scenario school, the observers will be seated and ready for the lesson to start, bang on time, and with little regard for what you have done before the lesson began. For example, it may be that you were on playground duty before the lesson and, despite your best efforts to reschedule the rota with your colleagues, you enter the classroom at the same time as your children. You then find yourself scrambling around for your own copy of the lesson plan, while trying to get the projector to come on, and igniting the whiteboard with your well thought out mental oral starter.

By now, the three extra bodies at the back of the room have already started making notes. These revolve around your head 'unprepared and unorganised'. The children are seated, and you begin your input, just as the teaching assistant walks through the door with her cup of tea in a non-standard issue, regulation, sealed lid cup and announces she has mislaid her lesson plan. You shuffle your copy into her hands and watch her go sit with the wrong group. Again, three pencils are positively smoking in unison as they make spurious notes. You've already primed a few children to ask questions and, remembering your no-hands up rule, you fire out a question to show learning is happening. At this point, things are going as well as can be expected given you are flying by the seat of your pants, because you now have no lesson plan to refer to.

You show the main lesson objective on the board and explain to the children what they will do for the session. Carefully, you explain every task to each table and make sure everyone knows what the vast array of colourful, laminated, and carefully constructed resources are for. After seeking clarification from each table that they understand, you set each group off and go sit with the very unfamiliar group, as allocated on your plan. Before you begin, you are sure to make eye contact with your teaching assistant and ensure she knows that she is currently sitting with wrong group, and you'd like her to move to the correct group. (NOW PLEASE!)

As the lesson unfolds, you and your group are actively engaged in the pre-prepared activity, and there is some feeling of understanding and excitement as you allow some active learning talk. At this stage, you glance around the class. Your two tops groups are working away, chatting about the task, and helping one another learn. Big tick to you. Your middle group appears to be struggling and the teaching assistant is currently sharpening pencils at the bin. As you leave your group to check all is okay, one member of the observers sits at the top group table, a second sits exactly where the teaching assistant should be, and the third takes your seat as soon as you have stood up.

Once again, you try to get the teaching assistant's attention, so you can throw her your best 'What the hell are you doing?' stare. She refuses to make eye contact.

As you wander around the classroom making essential check-ins with each group, you hear, almost in unison, the killer question from the observers, 'So what are you doing here and what are you learning from it?'

As you hang around, like the bad smell usually omitted from Dennis in the less able group, you desperately try to listen out for some sort of intelligent, valid, and relevant response. 'Don't know' comes the response. 'Just doing the thing with this other thing and trying to make forty-two'. Brilliant! Three hours of planning summed up in one sentence. The killer question from across the class, 'Does Sir normally sit with you and help you work?' You cross everything as your arse tightens and sweat pours down your back. Please just say yes. Like a bolt of lightning, you hear the immediate response, 'No, he normally marks books while we play on the iPad'. Brilliant, busted by a seven-year-old! Lesson shot to pieces!

School number two – the lesson:

Of course, not all observed lesson plans are to be feared. In some schools, the ideal best case scenario school, the lesson observation is…well, just another lesson.

You start your lesson with a motivational, inspired, and interactive lesson input. Just as this unfolds and everyone is chatting away, the door gently opens, two apologetic leaders walk in, and carefully find a seat. They glance at the board and listen to the learning. After a non-intrusive show of your five fingers counting down to one, all the children stop, and you ask them to share something new. As the chit chat begins and the leaders move around the room, everyone is talking about what they just learned in the opening introduction.

You glance over at both leaders, smiling at one another, making notes.

With the class fully engaged with you, you explain today's learning objective and each other's group task. As you move around the room for confirmation, each table repeats what they are expected to do and tell one another what their range of resources are there for. Your teaching assistant is poised and ready, sat with the high achievers and ready for them to challenge her knowledge. And you, you are sat in the middle of the class between two equally able groups.

As the lesson unfolds there is the usual learning chatter going on and, as you glance around, you see engaged children and more importantly, the teaching assistant engaged in her group and challenging their responses. The two senior leaders are floating from table to table and making polite enquiries with each child. There are notes being taken, these seem to be in the form of quotations from children or feedback from leading questions.

When the lesson reaches the mid-point, you decide upon a well-timed mini-plenary. Here you will just take a pit-stop, ensure everyone is on task, and understanding what to do. As you move round each table, the groups feedback what they have done and why. As well as telling you how they are going about problem solving. The teaching assistant feeds back some quotations from her table, and you fill the rest of the class in about what's been going on at your two tables. You are satisfied with the pit-stop, so learning begins again with a count-down to lesson end warning.

As you move swiftly along, your two tables are finished, and you see other children wrapping up their tasks. Now is the time to gather some much-needed feedback based on your learning objective. You mention some pre-prepared questions which will challenge today's learning and move around the groups looking for suitable responses. As you move around the class, you notice your two visitors have already left. Silently and without disruption. They have observed enough of your session to meet their own requirements.

Lesson feedback:

In all my years, I never, ever entered a feedback session without the first question being, 'So, how do you think that went?' This must be in some lesson observation bible somewhere, which is only ever read by those in senior leader positions. I never entered a feedback session and was asked, 'How are you?' or even a jovial 'Don't worry, no one died, it's all over now'. Anyway, what's more relaxing after an observation than the question, 'How do you think that went?'

School number one – lesson feedback:

You deliver your response to, *'How do you think it went?'* as best as you can. Given you taught a lesson straight after that one and it's now lunchtime and you haven't stopped to even analyse the output at this point. While delivering your response, you acknowledge elements of the lesson which maybe didn't go to plan or could have been improved. You try to emphasize all the good teaching and learning you noted, while accepting that until you mark the books, you can't really comment on the overall output.

After delivering your best assessment of the lesson, emphasising all along you have yet to see the output, you await further questions. What you don't expect is a barrage of questions and what-ifs. In my experience, these can go something like:

'Was there a reason you came into your lesson unprepared?'

'Well, I wasn't so much unprepared as just returning from…'

'Can you tell me why your teaching assistant arrived into the lesson late, holding a cup of hot tea, and unsure where she was meant to be?'

'Well, I have spoken to her before about using a safe-seal mug, and she was given a lesson plan yesterday. As to why she was…'

'So, it's common practise for her to bring hot tea into a lesson?'

'No, that's not what I was alluding to, it's just..'

'It seemed to us, looking at your plan anyway, she sat with the wrong group. Why is this?'

'Well, as you will have noted, I did give her my plan and…'

'Would you say she is unprepared generally?'

'No, I wouldn't…'

'Okay so moving on, do you usually leave your teaching assistant with the harder elements of the task?'

'No, I move her around, so she sits with a different group…'

'It's just she seemed to struggle, and you seemed to have sat with the lower ability children for the first time this term'.

'Well, no, we share the groups and I rotate...'

'Oh, one of the children mentioned that you never usually sit with them, and this made us think you'd planned this just for today'.

'Sorry, one child said...'

'Moving on, as we are short of time. It seems the children didn't really understand their tasks and the overall lesson objective. How do you think they did looking at their work?'

'Well, as I haven't yet had the time to view the output, I am not really...'

'Oh, you haven't looked yet? Do you think you're unprepared?'

'No. I had to teach a lesson straight after, tidy the room from the previous lesson, and hand...'

The conversation then tends to lead on to various elements of the lesson which were seen as good. Good range of resources, good classroom management, good subject knowledge and relevant, age-related content. For every good will usually be what is termed as an 'associated development point'. These will range from thing you cannot control, in this case your teaching assistant, to the things you can. A more detailed plan (Really?), a group consisting of mixed ability children, clearer and more defined instructions, and larger font on the whiteboard (Yes really!).

In the end you leave the session feeling less of a teacher and, at best, a half decent babysitter. You will reflect on the development points and soon forget the good elements. As the day rolls on, you'll get more and more annoyed with your teaching assistant. I mean how many times does she need to be told about hot drinks in the classroom? And the responses from the children which, quite frankly, made you look like you let the whole class run feral on a day-to-day basis.

In these schools, lesson observations are hard, full-on, and regular. Amid the 'It's all for your personal and professional development', you can slowly see any pay increase slip away. It's ok though, at least only you and the teaching assistant know how bad it went. Now for a quick word with her along the lines of 'Let's keep this to us and move on'. Except she is already in the staffroom discussing your very slow, but obvious, mental breakdown.

School number two – lesson feedback:

You begin to deliver your response to 'How do you think it went?' with confidence and clarity, because in these schools, the feedback session was planned into your timetable, and you were given time to reflect and review your work. As you deliver your feedback there are no interruptions, just random note taking, eye to eye contact, and a genuine interest in your feedback. Of course, you are asked to discuss what you think the children learned during the session. Your response to this is based on work, therefore factual and books can be shared to emphasise your points. As the observers view the work produced, they make note and leave you to continue. As you continue to dissect the lesson, careful notes are being made. You, the consummate professional, focus on your own development points. You wish there were time to sit with all groups. You are worried the lower ability group felt too challenged, but you know you need to push them. You think the top activity was too easy, as you noted they finished earlier than you would have liked. Finally, you acknowledge that the overall objective was very broad, but this was addressed in the individual objectives on you plan.

Considering all your input, you are then given feedback.

While it is noted that some of your points were valid, you are told to consider more the positive elements of the lesson, of which there were many. Your input was clear, concise, and relevant and the associated questions were pitched at just the right level. To add to this, you are informed the range of resources you selected were relevant, innovative, and well received by each group. While it is noted that, yes, the lower ability task did prove to be too hard, you are congratulated for your faith that the children would at least try, which they did. During a walk round of the class, each of the leaders noted just the correct amount of talk for learning and engagement from all. It was noted your teaching assistant seemed well placed, but it could be worth the teacher spending more time with that group to really push the learning on. Finally, it is noted the overall objective seemed unclear to some, but that it was correctly aligned to the lesson and the activities taking place. Your feedback ends with some development points. You are advised to be less harsh on yourself and remember the lessons need to be fun for all, including you. You are told to consider your adult support subject knowledge, and this should guide where they are placed. It is suggested that a revisit to the lesson objective-sooner rather than later could be a wise idea, and this lesson may need a follow-up.

Overall, you leave satisfied that you know your class, your teaching is suitably relevant, and you have the right amount of faith in yourself to teach a good lesson.

There appear to be no set pro-forma or standard approach to lesson observing. I myself have, as a subject leader, observed lessons. I have been in schools where no warning is given, and observers just arrived mid-lesson. I have also been in schools where fair notice is given, and time slots are agreed with the teacher. The latter always making for the best observation. It seems to me that if lesson observations are mandatory, and they are, and are solely carried out for the purposes of school and teacher development, then there should be a standard process put in place for all schools which forms part of any Ofsted inspection.

Do lesson observations make a difference? Do they vastly impact the teaching and learning? More importantly, do they improve pupil outcomes? Well, for the duration of the lesson being observed, yes, yes, and yes again. In the long run, who is to say they do or do not? It would be nice to think that teachers value their own professional integrity enough to always teach to the best of their ability, and to the limit of their subject knowledge. Do all teachers teach at 100%, five days a week? No, I don't believe so. Teachers have off days, too. Personal lives such as break ups, arguments, illness, death, and divorce get in the way. Yet every day the teacher arrives with their painted-on smile ready to go. Teachers are not robots, programmed to perform to a set of standards, irrespective of their own lives. Like every job, teachers need constant development, on the job training, and professional guidance. These are the things which make the difference in the class. Is being observed the best way to impact on pupil outcomes? It has to be acknowledged that if the answer to this question is 'no', then what other way is there? Video capture observations? I don't know. Every teacher can create a perfect lesson and a faultless lesson plan when they know they are being observed. Some don't have to and are what is seen as the 'best they can be' all the time. Some teachers crumble at the very thought of being observed, so the opposite outcome is achieved. Not everyone can or will perform under intense observation. This is by no means to say these teachers crumble in class every day.

The best thing any teacher can do, in my experience, is to be natural. I know this is harder to do when you're being observed, specifically in those cases where is feels like there is some hidden agenda to the observation. Or the headteacher is on some sort of mission to grind your soul and spirit. I look back at some of my best observations and the ones I took the most from where the ones I felt relaxed in. Yes, I tweaked the plan, changed the resources and switched my groups around, but generally I took a relaxed approach. The finest teaching comes from being relaxed, comfortable, and secure in your own practise. It will never feel normal to be watched while you work. But as any prospective or current teacher knows, it's part of the job when you work in a school. The best observers will give welcome feedback, make powerful observations about you, and your children, and provide ample opportunities for you to develop. In the end, you were given the job based on a lesson observation. Once you accept this is how your work life will continue, the more relaxed and accepting you will be and the more natural your observations will become.

Ofsted

Your performance can make or break this school.
No pressure, just be your best

As a child in school, I don't recall more than one adult in my class at any one time. This is not to say other adults were not in the class, I just don't recall the permanent presence of a teaching assistant. Was this even a 'thing' in the 80s and 90s? As a child I was always aware when another adult entered the room. Unlike today, you'd stop and stare at the opening door, even stand out of your chair until the entering adult gave the nod for you to sit. When another adult entered the room, they either went straight to the teacher and had a close ear conversation or, more amusing for the children, they would blurt out the Christian name of your teacher – 'Good afternoon, Francis... Sorry, Mr Davies, how are the class today?' From memory, I had one teacher and the interruption of visiting adults was minimal.

It's very rare today, specifically in primary schools, to see just the one adult in a classroom. Depending on the class dynamic, there could be as many as three adults in one class, for the duration of the day. It goes without saying, one of these people will be a classroom teacher. The planner of activities and lessons, the presumed font of all knowledge, and the person with whom the buck stops. To add to this, there will usually be a teaching assistant. The role of the teaching assistant varies, for many, many reasons. Too many to go into. Ideally, they are there to help facilitate and deliver a lesson to children of differing abilities with the purpose of aiding the teacher in the delivery of all learning. Rather than someone else requiring direction, observing, and monitoring.

A third person could be a 1-2-1 support assistant, also known as a Pupil -Support Assistant. In the classroom where, for whatever reason, a pupil requires 1-2-1 support, there will be a third body who is solely there for the purposes of one child. The purpose of a Pupil Support Assistant is to support learning and teaching within the curriculum and the personal development of learners with additional support needs. This person must not be confused with, or treated like, another teaching assistant. They will require in-depth knowledge of upcoming lessons, activities, learning objectives, and outcomes weeks in advance for the sole purpose of ripping them apart, rewriting them, and delivering them in their own style. Are they expected to plan their own lessons tailored just for that one child? Not in my experience. You are, after all, the teacher.

In addition to the above forementioned adults, you could even go as far as saying it is not uncommon to have periods of time where there could be five or six adults in the classroom at one time. The teacher, the teaching assistant, the pupil support assistant, and two or three additional adults observing a lesson. This point brings me nicely to the other adults who have the ability to enter your lesson at any given time, with minimal notice but maximum impact… The dreaded Ofsted inspector.

Mention the word Ofsted to any headteacher, deputy head, or teacher and it will strike fear into their very core. Ofsted are: the Office for Standards in Education whose role it is to inspect and regulate services that care for children and young people. Ofsted make sure organisations providing education, training, and care, do so to a high standard for every child and adult receiving said education and training. This being said, you would expect any school to welcome Ofsted inspectors with open arms, cups of tea, cake, and a welcoming smile. The reality is that this is not the case and never has been, at least in my experiences. Ofsted are feared by all school staff. I have yet to know a school who have welcomed Ofsted in any way, shape, or form. The mere mention of the 'O-Word' can send the nicest of head, teachers, and secretaries into meltdown. To the outsider (non-teaching staff / non-school workers) why the big drama? If Ofsted are just coming to check procedures and that good learning is taking place, why the big fuss? As an insider, it remains the case 'They are here to judge me, my classroom, my children, and my ability to teach'.

While recently the procedures for a visit have changed, I can only reflect on my own experiences at the time I write. Ofsted inspectors will usually give a school forty-eight hours' notice maximum, or twenty-four hours' notice minimum of an impending visit. Please do not mistake the word 'visit' for anything else other than 'inspection'. They are, after all, called Ofsted inspectors. I used the word 'usually' in the previous sentence, but realistically, Ofsted have the power to go into schools without any notice if they feel it is necessary. This is usually the case if they have received serious concerns about a school. For example, something relating to safeguarding. It is normal for the lead inspector to phone the school to announce a visit around about 10 a.m. the day before. The point of the call, apart from acting as a prewarning to all, is for the inspector to explain the purpose of their visit to the head, discuss the school context, and put in place arrangements for who they will meet upon arrival the following day. On the day of the visit, the inspectors will not normally arrive before 10 a.m. or leave after 4 p.m. I have experienced inspectors who arrived at 8:30 a.m. and decided to just hang-back in the staffroom until they were ready.

In my experience, as soon as a visit is announced, the headteacher will gather all staff in one place at the earliest possible time. I have seen meetings in staffrooms during whole school assembly, meetings in the hall after lunch, and even extended play times while the head gathers everyone together to announce the news. Once everyone has been informed, that is usually when panic mode kicks in. Officially, Ofsted don't want schools to do any prep pre-visit. They want the day-to-day business of the school to continue and if they require any documentation to aid their inspection, it should be randomly produced on the day from its normal safe place.

The reality is, as a teacher, you will go into a tailspin looking through all your planning folders. You want the reassurance that, should anyone ask you for evidence of planning, all of your paperwork is present, up to date, annotated to show evidence of progression, and planning cohesion. As well making sure there is differentiation, adult intervention, and support notes evident. To add to this, you will spend however long it takes to ensure every single book, even those topic and French books, is marked with suitable and relevant pupil feedback. It is not uncommon for afternoon sessions of science, history, and art to be shelved and substituted with feedback to marking session the afternoon before the inspection. On many occasions I pushed aside planned sessions to hand out books and inform children that we were all going to look back through our books and ensure all teacher comments have ben responded to.

In the event I was asked why, I would say, 'This is to help me when it comes to writing your reports and it makes sure I can help you all with any difficulties you may be having later in the week'. I mean, I was never likely to say, 'Children, grab your books, respond to all of my marking because Ofsted are coming tomorrow and I have an arse that needs covering in glory', was I? Once this was done, the final hurdle, when it came to marking at least, was to ensure all children's comments were then acknowledged, relating back to the comment made by them. So much easier at the time, harder when it was retrospective, and you needed to justify what work came next. I never worked with one colleague who managed to stay on top of their marking or their pupil feedback. In the event I did, they were never happy, better off for it, or liked!

Once your books were in some state of readiness and you were convinced your plans were annotated, consistent, and reflective of the work in books, it was on with the next job on the ever-increasing list. It is my understanding that Ofsted no longer require any pre-written planning, self-evaluation, or other documentation. I have also been told school leaders expect these to be requested and should always be to-hand if requested. Another change since my days in school is Ofsted will not require teachers to prepare any lesson plans or examples of assessments, nor put up any displays for the visit. It is important to note this was not the case when I was teaching. It was obligatory in every school I taught in that once the visit had been announced, every display in the school had to be made perfect and ready for inspection. Teachers would take responsibility for the classroom displays and an army of teaching assistants would tend to the communal and hall displays. All hands went to deck, stapling torn and tattered boarders, ensuring each display had a double boarder and bold title. Pieces of children's best work photocopied, enlarged, laminated, marked, and highlighted so they could be the pride of the relevant display. In addition, you had to find the examples of work which may have been not so great but got marks for trying. So, this could also be marked, laminated, and backed for the display. Throughout the school the echo of the guillotine running back and forth, the clattering of drawing pins, and snapping of wall staplers was deafening as bodies busied themselves. Desperate to present the perfectly colourful, diverse, well-rounded displays for all to see.

Display attended to and strict instructions issued not to touch, marking and feedback up to date, and planning evident and annotated, it's on to the next job, safeguarding. Where is your evidence that child safety is number one? Have you, the class teacher, got a copy of the school safeguarding policy? Have you read it, understood it, signed it, and can you recount it should you be asked? What measures do you take to ensure your children are safe at all times, both in your classroom and around the school? Can you tell me what steps are in place to prevent your children from leaving the building? When was the most recent breach of this policy? What did you do once you were made aware of it? Who is your designated safeguarding officer? What is the procedure if a child makes a disclosure to you? Can you name the signs of neglect and how you'd deal with them for a child in your care? Answers to all of these questions and many more need to be digested and remembered in the event you are asked one or more of them during the visit.

In addition to the above, it may be beneficial for you to become familiar with other school documentation. Such as the school improvement plan (SIP), behaviour policy, and the last Ofsted report. Every teacher should be aware of the documents. Very few are, because, to be honest, it does not affect your day-to-day teaching, digesting, and absorbing all the information. It is expected you will know what your most recent SIP looks like, where it is kept, when it was agreed, and what your part in it is. The reality is, SIPs are huge, sometime twenty plus page documents. They can cover routines, relationships, pupil outcomes, curriculum changes, leadership goals, attendance, behaviour …Shall I go on?

This being the case, it is not unusual that the SIP, once agreed, will be placed in your pigeonhole for you to read, absorb, sign, and return in usually a very short time period. Most teachers will skim read it, sign and date it, and return it, never to be read or seen again. The truth is senior leaders need to know the SIP inside out. However, teachers just need an overview, an understanding of key priorities for the upcoming year, or the upcoming term, so they know what they are aiming for. Prior to the inspection, find a copy, look at the overarching targets, pinpoint what this term's priority is, and you should convince anyone asking. Behaviour policies are usually set at the start of the year and reviewed depending on the dynamics of your school. Again, what is the school's policy? How do you apply it, and do the children know it? Get these three sorted, and you should cover off any questions asked.

With regards to the last Ofsted inspection, well this you should know. It is one of the deciding factors why you chose the school, is it not? As a teacher, you want to demonstrate you know what the last report findings were, specifically where the areas of improvement were. If these related to behaviour, classroom management, and safeguarding then you need to know and be able to demonstrate how you are addressing them. It's worth mentioning, if you fail child protection your school is automatically placed into inadequate (at my time of teaching, at least).

Ofsted inspections can last two days. These will most likely be the two most stressful days you ever encounter as a teacher. You will be told to relax and be yourself. You'll be told, 'Just make sure you teach your best lesson'. And, 'They are not judging you; you have nothing to worry about'. None of these are achievable. It's abnormal to feel relaxed when an inspector is present in school because everything else is so fake. The perfect displays, the male teachers who suddenly discover ties and jackets (I always wore a three-piece suit every day of my teaching career), the interactive teaching areas that popped up overnight, and the perfectly polite lunchtime supervisors. The two days are fearsome and stressful, and I've never experienced anything but.

The fear is not knowing what is happening in the background. If an inspector enters your class, yes, it's daunting, but at least you know. You know what they want to hear, want to see, and you know they will interact at some point. Ofsted interaction, by the way, is terrifying! It only takes one child and one response to bring the whole façade tumbling down. My worst experience of this was in my third year of teaching. I was halfway through a geography lesson. We were establishing whether places in the world were countries, cities, or towns. Random place names were shown on the interactive board, and all the children had to do was come to the board and write next to a named place the word 'country', 'city' or 'town'. This was an end of unit assessment activity and to be honest, I did not worry when the inspector walked in. He asked a child what we were doing and why and they managed to reply sensibly. As my next child approached the board and selected the United Kingdom as their choice, I sat back confidently, knowing this child would identify correctly that the U.K was a country. The inspector, along with the rest of the class, waited. At that point, the child held the interactive stylus and began to be write on the board, in nice bold letters, C . . . U . . . N . . . I have never leapt from my chair so quickly to disarm a child from what could have been a dangerous weapon!

As I looked across the class, I asked said child, 'What where you about to write?' The child responded, 'Country, Sir, the U.K is a country'. Sweat dripping from every pore, I applauded the child and encouraged them to sit down. In another example of Ofsted interaction being the poison chalice, an inspector asked one of my children, 'Are your lessons always this nice and fun?' To which the child responded, 'Well yesterday we had to respond to marking all afternoon and when we had finished, we went out to play rounders in our normal clothes'. The only thing out of a teacher's control during an Ofsted inspection is the children.

There can be no denying that Ofsted inspections are stressful, tiresome, and draining. The run up is as stressful as the event itself, and the two days can feel like a fortnight. It feels as though every inch of you, your teaching, your knowledge, and your professionalism is being hung out to dry. The inspectors will move around the school like deathly shadows, leaving their mark on everything and anything they see. Your books will be scrutinised, your data analysed. Your children will be spoken to during lessons, lunchtimes, and playtimes. Parents will be spoken to, lunchtime supervisors will be on edge, the whole school is like a cauldron just simmering away, ready to boil over at any time. During all of this, the advice you will be given: Just act like they are not there. Carry on regardless, we are doing just fine. Frustratingly, not all Ofsted inspectors will have had the experience of being teachers. And this always stuck in my claw. I was being judged and observed by someone who had never felt the stress and pressures I felt on a day-to-day basis.

Ofsted inspections are performances. They are a showcase of you and your school at your very best. You showcase your ability, knowledge, understanding, and your confidence. As well as your ability to plan engaging, interactive, and fun lessons where every learning style is addressed. You perform for some unknown authority figure who may walk in at the start, the middle, or the end of your lesson and base their judgements of you on ten or twenty minutes of observation. Based on this, you may be judged as outstanding, good, requires improvement, or inadequate. The weight of this responsibility is overwhelming. Imagine being judged as outstanding, only to find your overall visit was classified as 'requires improvement'. Worse still, imagine all that preparation, work, effort, and time, only to be judged as inadequate. Despite outstanding displays, exceptional behaviour from children, and a warm and welcoming environment, just twenty minutes can bring it all crashing down.

As I previously mentioned, Ofsted have changed their approach and their requirements since my experiences of them. This being said, I still do not know many teachers or leaders who welcome the visit. Some will profess, 'Oh, we have nothing to fear. We know we are doing well'. While others will say, 'Well it's not me being judged, it's the school'.

Regardless, they still strike fear and terror into teachers. I don't see the fear ever going away, and maybe it shouldn't. I no longer know. The best thing I could ever advise is: Answer any question honestly. If you know, you know. If you don't know, can't recall, or have just plain forgot, then tell them and go find the answer. You can't blag it, so why bother? Can one bad Ofsted end your career? No. Can a series of bad inspections? More likely. Specifically, if the finger always points your way. The best you can hope is, particularly in the early days, you dodge the inspection in whatever school you are in. When it happens, be the best person you can and do your bit. Finally, make sure you have children who know how to spell, specifically the word country!

After School / Lunchtime Clubs

If everyone takes on a club, our children will soar in no time

When I look back at my childhood and think about school, I can't seem to recall ever wanting, or needing to, turn up early and / or stay late. My school days were simple. Leave home with enough time to spare that I can walk to school, usually with my brother or some local friends from the street, via the shop for some sweets. Arriving at school about fifteen minutes before the bell. This was ample enough time for a quick kick around or chat with the girls. Then saunter into class and await the arrival of my teacher. The end of the day wasn't too dissimilar. The end of day bell would ring, my books, pencil case and other belongings were scooped into a bag and as I ran out of class, I'd collect my coat from its peg, and run like a madman out of the school gate. Normally to avoid the school bully, or to catch-up with my brother and his friends so I could look cool walking home with older boys.

Today, for some, school starts earlier and finishes much later than I ever remember. Today's schools offer a range of clubs and activities, meaning some school days can run from 7.30 a.m. to 5.30 p.m., much to the dismay of many teachers.

Schools strive to be seen as the hub of their communities. Offering a wide range of activities for their children and parents, throughout the year. These range from: Breakfast club, meet the teacher sessions, P.T.A auctions, and curriculum health checks. Some schools offer out their space as community hubs and even stretch to parish meetings, if affiliated with a local church. Seemingly, there is nothing a school won't do to be at the heart of the community.

If you're lucky, you as a teacher will escape most of the above. In my experience, breakfast clubs are usually run by teaching assistants or helpful parents desperate not to be separated from their little darlings for any longer than is needed. Other clubs can and do run during the school day, and usually are run for the parents. So, you will not be involved, no matter how hard you may try.

It is more common practise now for teachers to be asked to run a club. This could be a lunchtime or an after-school club. Both times when you'd more likely want to be marking, planning, assessing or, maybe, just maybe, grabbing a bite to eat. As an ECT it's almost frowned upon if you don't volunteer to run an after-school club. It's like you're saying, 'I really don't want to be a part of this community'. This is where you scramble round your brain for all of those extra things you brought to the school, all those months ago in your interview. Although, from my time, if you were an ECT you were not required to run a club.

Typically, clubs, be them after school or lunchtime, have one purpose, to contain the worst behaved children for the longest period of time in one place. Lunchtime clubs are not set-up to provide extra learning provision or focussed teaching time. Lunchtime clubs are set-up to give options to the worst behaved, most trouble causing, and problematic children in the school. Keep them contained and contain the impact of their madness, right? The options are simple: Pick a lunchtime club, be it indoors or outdoors, and at least be in one place for the whole hour. Or play outside with your friends and risk being put on report for fighting, bullying, or swearing. In the end, these children may not be popular or even liked, but they know the better option.

Inevitably, lunchtime clubs see football and other sports related club's set-up and run so the hyperactive, mindless bullies can focus their energy on kicking and throwing balls. While their playground buddies take a rest from being hit, sworn at, and used as punchbags. After school clubs serve the same purpose, but with more of a babysitting element. In my experiences of running both types of clubs in a range of subject areas, it's a lose-lose situation for the teacher. The choices being: Give up your lunchtime to hold a club for the rowdy or give up an hour after school to babysit the rowdy, the geeky, and the neediest of children Either way, you won't get chance to eat, plan, or mark any books for the duration.

At some point during the first term, if not on that first inset day even, you'll be presented with an email, a staff room notice board announcement, or even an agenda at a staff meeting which proposes it's time for everyone to think of which club they would like to run in term two. Either after school or at lunchtime. I've rarely seen any communication which offers a choice. It's always, 'Which club would you like to run?' Or 'Which club do you want to suggest?' Using the words 'like' and 'want' to make it feel like it's your suggestion rather than having thumbscrews turned at a vast rate.

In some cases, a list will be passed round for immediate sign up. Pressure! And in others, you will need to complete a table, which is already attached to the staffroom door, by a given date.

Immediately, you are wracking your brain for the easiest to run, minimal effort, and lowest turnout club you can think of. Ideally, inside – nobody wants to commit to rugby club or football club. Automatically ensuring you will be doomed to an outside activity once a week, come what may. You know your school is looking for ways to improve writing outcomes, as well as encourage boys to read. So, you opt to run a lunchtime reading club, ideal. You head back to the signup sheet, only to see that not only have all the lunchtime slots filled up, but that someone as also had your exact thought and opted for a reading club. Now you're in trouble. This actually looks serious. Your name isn't down, you are, by default, committed to after school and have no discernible skills or latent desire to run any after school club.

After much soul searching, you opt for computer club. You know the laptops are ancient, take ten minutes to fire up and run at the speed of a blind tortoise. That would seem the most likely club to get fewest sign-ups and be cancelled first, due to either poor attendance or equipment failure. Computer club it is.

Dutifully, you add your name to the ever-growing list and there it is. You've just given up another hour of your time to school work and surrounding yourself with the very children you spend six hours a day trying to escape from. Before you have chance to let it sink in, that you have now openly given up another hour of your time, a newsletter is printed and all the lunchtime and after school clubs are printed and sent home to parents, eagerly waiting to unload their children on you for another hour. Upon close inspection of your club offering, now committed to print, you note there is a small footnote stating, 'A maximum of twenty children allowed per club. This will be decided upon a first come, first allocated basis'. Twenty! Twenty children per club?! That equates to two thirds of your daily class number. This isn't so much a club, more of a large gathering! It's ok though. You are safe in the knowledge that Spanish club, chess club, art club, and the more welcoming Lego club are also on offer and seem far more appealing to the children you know.

Within days of the newsletter going out, you find yourself inundated with permission slips, well in excess of the 'twenty child' limit. On a daily basis, they arrive in the register, along with eager children inundating you with questions which, until this point, you haven't even considered. 'Can we bring our own devices?', 'Will we be designing and making our own games?', 'Will we be learning about Minecraft?', and 'What night will it be?' Your head is spinning with the absolute fury that parents even dare sign their children up. You bat off all the questions with, 'It will be on the letter which will go out to your parents'. So, to add more to your ever growing after school club list, you now have to write a letter.

Out of sheer desperation, you go ask a colleague what they are planning to do, how will they address all the questions, and what night were they planning on holding their club.

You grab the closest colleague, who somehow managed to get zero requests for their proposed chess club, and they smile. Not a huge smile, one of those crooked mouth, smug arse smiles. You know the ones that scream, 'Ha-Ha!' without actually saying the words.

Useless! It's ok, the staff meeting is tonight. You'll gauge the feeling for what everyone else is doing at that point.

Over the course of the six minutes, it was given at the staff meeting, the following was made clear: After school clubs will need to be purposeful and meaningful, with educational objectives. Each club will require some level of planning, this is down to the teacher's discretion. But these plans will need submitting, evaluated, at the end of the club. Clubs will run for one term. Teachers must make sure the children are selected on a first come, first served basis while also giving priority to those children who have fallen behind in the chosen subject. Including those from less able groups. Finally, teachers will be responsible for writing and sending out their own club letters, as well as registration on the evening of each club. This is not a job to be done by the office staff who are far too busy to be managing this for you. (Because you are not busy enough, it would seem!) So, with the first club just three nights away, you have children to select, consider all aspects other than first come, first served, letters to write and send, permission slips to collect, a register to make and…oh yes, a lesson plan to write.

By some miracle, you have selected the group, sent them home with letters, and have most of the slips collected in. Using your teacher discretion, you have planned the first session and have not managed to look beyond that point, at this stage. Right now, you know who is coming and have a vague idea what you will teach. You have a register and the vain hope that by time the actual laptops turn on and children get logged in, it will be time to leave.

Leaving the excuse of 'poor, tired laptops' as the reason nothing actually got done. Thus, leaving your lesson plan ready for next week. All this for a one hour club, which you don't actually want any part of!

The evening of your club, the laptops arrive and are wheeled outside your classroom well before the 3.20 p.m. bell. You see there is a note attached to the trolley. This is it. You pray for a note saying, 'Unfortunately several of the laptops are unable to be used because…'

As you tear off the post-it you read a message from the I.T technician, 'All laptops updated, debugged, and ready for use'. Brilliant!

In all likelihood, the children attending will be a mix of two requirements. First, the requirement to stay at school for an extra hour, through choice or not, so the parent or parents can delay the inevitability of taking back their little angel one hour later than usual. In these cases, the child cares not what they can learn, or add to their ever-growing computing knowledge. But more about zoning out in front of a screen where they may or may not be able to play a game for the next hour (a.k.a dimwits). Second, will be the requirement to take the opportunity to use this extra hour to boost their knowledge and understanding with the sole purpose of being able to run home and boast about what they have just learned. In these cases, the child has a need to learn (a.k.a geeks). Hence you have a need to plan and teach a specific skill. Regardless of requirement or ability, you are expected to teach and, with all of the computing equipment up and running, that is what you do.

Bringing any level, calm, or order to a club, is the best part of the hour wasted. This rule does not apply to the lucky teacher who chose film-club. The children in that club will arrive on time, take their seats, and settle within minutes. They want the maximum amount of time to see the scheduled film. In all other clubs it can be very different. Regardless of the club, in my experience, children will see this time as 'not normal school time', or really see the advantages in the words 'after school'. Despite your best-efforts, children will turn up late, arrive eating snack, arrive with some sort of begrudging attitude because their parents have made them stay, or not arrive at all.

The latter of these children can usually be seen out of the window heading for the gate or kicking some poor soul's head in, in the corner of the field. As children arrive, calm and order are not really in their minds. They want to catch-up with friends, chill out for the hour, or do the minimal amount of work because, 'We've been working all day, Sir'. You, on the other hand, clearly have not been working all day and really want to make this next hour about nothing but work and marking! As you bring some relative calm to the club, you'll soon notice time is quickly passing by and some children did actually come to learn, unfortunately.

Teachers will take differing approaches to after school clubs. Some will continue the teacher façade and insist on peace, calm, and work. Time wasted in my view, but a sure-fire tactic to assure dwindling numbers over the coming weeks. Some teachers will ensure the club is relaxed with the right amount of noise, productivity, and engagement to justify the children staying and, hopefully, returning week after week. Other teachers will open the door, ask the children to sit, and entertain themselves with a pre-determined task, leaving them to get on and catch-up on the days marking. The strategy to after school club really does depend on the activity, the teacher, and the children attending.

I always viewed school clubs, specifically after school club, as a huge infringement on my time and approached each and any club with resentment. How dare they ask me for more of my time! This resentment wasn't aimed so much at the children. Well not in the first few minutes of the club. It wasn't aimed at the parents. Although there was always that collective of parents who used you as a babysitter so they could have that extra hour in Asda, Primark, or at the hairdressers. Mostly, my resentment was aimed at the school, the head who insisted these clubs go ahead, even my colleagues for agreeing with such enthusiasm to run their own clubs. (Butt-kissers!) The request to do clubs was voluntary, but as everyone agreed so enthusiastically, this became mandatory.

There was no remit, just 'pick a club for the term'. Yet everyone decided to opt for curricular subjects. With the exception of film club, which still annoys you because you didn't think of it. As the idea gathered momentum, the clubs required planning and lesson objectives. With this came the consideration of ability group management and behaviour strategies. Finally, you weren't allowed to specify specific year groups, or even exclude children who were badly behaved throughout the day. Meaning all age groups, all abilities, and all manner of attitudes could walk into the club. All of this meant extra management, responsibility, and work. It's hard not to feel resentment when you're asked to give up extra time. That one hour a week takes up three or four hours in preparation and assessment and for what? Parents to complain that the club isn't exciting enough, it finishes too late, or their child isn't learning anything. As with lots of areas in the job, you'll end up marking pieces of work no one will see, producing plans to sit inside a folder, and creating resources and activities no one will complete. But at the end, you can at least say you 'volunteered' for a club.

In the constant strive to be community friendly and at the heart of the community hub, schools will continue to offer services and support to their parents and children. This support will take many forms, at the core of which will always be the head teacher. Driving the club initiative through to the community, and the staff beating the drum until all involved comply. As a teacher you don't want to be the first to say no when the call comes to monitor the school disco, lead a forest school, or take an after-school club. The resentment aimed your way for doing so, is not worth it.

As such, these activities, and many more, soon become part of your normal working week. Marking, planning, and assessing takes a back seat to ensure you get the best out of the club or activity you 'volunteered' for. That being said, make the hour count. Pick a club you at least think will excite the children.

Dare to be bold with your ideas. Ignore the requirement to provide reading club, writing club, or homework club. If you don't like the idea, neither will the children and this makes attendance so much harder. Submit a suggestion knowing two things: Firstly, if you get the nod, it could be the most enjoyable and exciting hour of your week and the children's week. Secondly, if the idea is too bold, too extreme, or not really for our children, then by that time all the other clubs will have gone, and you may find yourself side-lined for clubs until next term. Which is great, because you'll be the first one to suggest film club!

The School Performance

Remember, you're not directing "The Titanic"
for God's sake

I had many an appearance in a school production, as a child. In infant school, I played the doctor in some odd stage version of 'Miss Polly had a Dolly'. While I don't remember how this came about, I do remember my excitement at being dressed in a white coat, plastic stethoscope, and a red plastic doctor's case. I had to rush onto stage, knock on a door, (Which wasn't there, it was a sound effect) and say, 'Put her straight to bed'. Then rush off again. Early signs there that I would have made a great NHS doctor! As I moved up through school, my roles became bigger. In junior school I was given the role of a shepherd in the nativity play back when schools still did traditional nativity plays. Unlike today where they include wise lobsters or roving reporters for the Bethlehem times.

I was so excited; shepherd was a big deal. I still remember to this day, all I had to do was walk on stage with my other two shepherds, point to the sky and say, 'Look, a star. Let's follow it'. Ok, not exactly propping up the whole play, but crucial information in the story, right? I don't recall what I wore, other than one of my mum's striped tea-towels on my head, secured and tied with a velvet chord – this was the 1980's after all. My moment came and I walked on carrying my fluffy toy sheep under my arm. In front of the whole school, my parents, and everyone else's parent's, I delivered my line. At the same time, I dropped my sheep, burst out crying, and ran off stage! I knew there and then; the shepherd life wasn't for me! I don't recall putting myself forward for any other parts in junior school, but I am certain I sung in the odd play or two and supported with scenery and back of shot roles.

My final shot at fame came in the senior school, where I felt more confident to assert my acting prowess and I volunteered for the role of Singing Bolshevik Robot. Looking back, I have no clue what sort of production this was, but playing the part of a radical, far-left revolutionary, it was obviously some deep and meaningful statement that I missed. I only volunteered because along with me, one of the other five robots was a girl I really fancied and hoped to spend more time with. This part, as with my other starring roles, went equally as well. I recall going on stage, in the background, of course, dancing the wrong routine, kicking the girl I fancied, and exiting stage the wrong way. Fair to say, my experiences of being on stage never really lit up Hollywood. More of a flickering candle on the windowsill, in a raging storm.

Alongside the many of the other things you are not taught or warned about while studying your teaching degree, is that at some point it will fall upon you to be responsible for a school play. Or to give them their proper name, 'End of term performance'. I am not sure when it happened, possibly while I was working hard in finance or retail trying to pay my mortgage. But the term 'school play' seems to have phased out and replaced with 'school production'. The very nature of the word makes you think of a theatrical work of art or a grand performance which includes music, acting, and stage direction. Let us not forget, we are talking about primary school children here! Everything seems to have become so...big! School performance, end of term prom, limousines and prom dresses, red carpets, and glitter balls. When I was at school, we had an end of term disco. You got your shirt signed, only after mid-day, had a disco, was really excited if it was a fancy-dress disco, brought

£1.00 for some crisps and a can of fizzy drink, and got to leave earlier than everyone else. Saying awkward goodbyes to teachers or running out the gates dressed as Superman while flicking Vs at the school building! Today everything is so grand and there is this expectation that this year will be the best year ever!

In truth, I never minded organising (Or should that be, producing?) the yearly school performance. I always found it was the most obscure, quiet, and least obvious children who gave the best performances. Yes, there were the obvious children who just had to get a part to appease Mum and Dad, or because they had the largest mouth and the most influence over their peers. Generally, in my experience, it wasn't these lovely little angels who gave their best. For me, it was those children who were genuinely surprised to be picked for a role. The ones who put themselves down as 'crowd' or 'background noise', who when given a major role, acted, sung, and danced their hearts out. For me, it will always be the memory of those children that make me smile when I think back to the productions I have been involved in, or organised...sorry, produced.

During my teaching carer I produced a whole range of productions. *The Jungle Book*, *Cinderella Rockerfella*, *Grease*, *Aladdin*, and some weird underwater pirate adventure I can't even recall the name of. It must be said there is nothing more equally frustrating and magical than organising an end of year production. Your vision is made up of many factors: A good script which the children will know or will have heard of, willing participants, a good variety of dialogue, dance, song, and the idea that the end result will provide a tear or two as your year 6 class demonstrate their excitement at leaving. As well as many happy memories they will take with them. Pulling off this vision has many, many obstacles.

Despite knowing that, wherever you are and whatever school you are in, the year will end with a school production. It's never considered early enough to warrant any decent amount of planning time. While every facet of every subject is planned within an inch of the working day, the end of year school production is not usually considered until at least term 5. If you're a year 6 teacher, it will fall to you to decide what the production will be, when it will be shown (Usually two evenings and one afternoon), who will be in it, when rehearsal time will be, and what members of staff will be involved. Add to this, making the tickets, designing, and making the posters and you're suddenly producing a localised Hollywood mega-pic.

If you're a two-form entry school, you do at least have the burden to share with your partner teacher. This means one evening after school, either in the classroom, or the pub, you'll have a chat about your ideas, argue who's is best, flip a coin for the deciding title, and spend the next pint or three deciding the logistics of when, where, and how. Collectively, you will decide who will help in the form of teaching assistants, where rehearsals will be, and when it will all kick off. The rehearsal 'when' element is a given. It will always be afternoon, as Math and English cannot be displaced. You also need to decide, how auditions will take place. In what seems like no time, you will have: production name, rehearsal times and days, helping hands, rehearsal place, and audition format. All you need now is the relevant budget to purchase a script, or the network of friends to be able to produce a script, CD, and song sheets for free. Very few schools like purchasing scripts.

The auditions:

Auditions for the school productions are, in short, a nightmare! Once you have managed to beg, borrow or buy a script with all that it contains (Prompt sheets, cast list, stage directions, musical note sheet, and CD), you then have to cast for your leading characters, supporting roles, background cast,

163

and scenery helpers. No longer can you pin up a cast list and allow children to pick who they want to be, because everyone wants to play the lead, the villain, or the good guy. Nobody wants to be a scenery hand, background crowd, or in charge of music (and those who do volunteer are encouraged by overzealous parents to 'get more involved'). What this then leads to is endless days and hours of an X-Factor type audition process. Before you know it, you have assumed the role of Simon Cowell, with your fellow teacher / judge Will.I.Am sat next to you, having to endure child after child try and deliver the simplest of lines in some ham-fisted, Hollywood style that neither suits the play, the role, or your ears.

Intelligent, bright, and enthusiastic children suddenly become incompetent and even with the simplest of directions fail them. You'll endure hours of,

'Stand on the spot, read lines three, four, six and seven to me, following the directions in the brackets'.

'What brackets? Where?'

'The ones after the character name, look, where it says 'shouting''.

'So, do I shout?'

'Yes, shout at me lines three, four, six, and seven'.

At this point, the child shouts so loud, the head burst in and scolds you for disturbing the old folk in their homes four miles away.

There will always, without any doubt, be arguments about who plays which role. Not just the children, but the adults, too. Ultimately you will end up with a lead boy and lead girl. Cinderella and Buttons, Danny and Sandy, Simba and Pumbaa…the list is endless. What this means is that you will try, in a two-form entry school, to pick lead roles equal to each class. Meaning equal amounts of children from each class get a role. This is fine, unless the teacher you work with, or you, think you have the better children in your class.

An all-out war will erupt, jeopardising the entire production. To add to this, don't forget the kids with pushy parents, supportive parents, deprived parents, and the kids whose parent may work at the school. All of them will want their say. Despite entering into this whole project with a clear vision and knowing deep down who will be who, you will always be compromised by some unknown factor beyond your control. I recall once being told to replace my choice of lead girl (Who was very expressive, an excellent reader, and amazing at learning lines) with a less-able child because her mum had called to say how upset her child was because, 'They always get pushed to the back, and never get lead roles'. Never get lead roles? In what? This is the only production they have been involved with! As a teacher, you'll never make the right choice. Auditions will become competitive, tiresome and painful to endure. There will always be a debate about who should get the lead role. The best thing you can do is go with your initial thoughts and take the backlash from all the parents, teachers, children, and everyone else who isn't involved in the production.

Rehearsals:

Probably the single, most painful part of organising any production is the rehearsals. Rehearsals are a constant battle with everyone involved. To start with, you have to allocate all rehearsal time into an already busy timetable. You, as the dedicated producer of the production, will need to tell everyone else, normally in a staff meeting or an email, where the rehearsals will take place, what days and times they will happen, who will be involved, how long they will take, and what lessons these will interrupt for all involved. Again, an easier task if you are in a two-form entry school as the decisions are all shared. Along with the blame for any disruption.

Once logistics are sorted, you have to convince your head why you have chosen specific time slots, let's say three afternoons per week as an example. Having decided to give you all the responsibility for the production, you would have thought scheduling would be included, but no. You will have to justify to your head, and possibly heads of subjects, too, why you have decided to put rehearsals in place of music, geography, history, and art. Sadly, 'Because these subjects mean less to me and my class than any other', or 'Because I'm crap at teaching them' is not a suitable response. The expectation will always be the same, if you are planning on using these timeslots for rehearsals then the children will need to make sure they make up any lost learning opportunities at a later date. Yes, because your class is full of budding musicians, artist, and archaeologists, you really won't want them to miss their calling in life!

In an ideal scenario, by the time rehearsals come around, you have already allocated roles to everyone involved. This will include your most treasured children who read with ease, express themselves perfectly, and will be fully dedicated to their lead role. As well as your background character roles, happy to be the bustling crowd, lurking stranger, policeman, and player of more than one role. There will always be the special children who you know will not read out aloud, will not express themselves verbally or physically, and show no interest in any kind of performance. But, not unlike sports day, have to be included. These will be the children who will become scenery managers -costume production assistants, and lighting and audio technicians. All this is, as previously mentioned, an ideal scenario. The reality is usually very different. Having already selected the most diverse, yet slightly biased cast that you can, you suddenly find that, when asked to perform, children will become shrinking violets, unable to speak in front of their peers. I cannot count how many times I organised the school production. Every time, the pattern was the same. Most of the rehearsal time will be spent handing out scripts, telling children to stop playing with the scripts, rolling them up, or curling them over. To add to this, there will be so much starting and stopping that by time a scene is practised and perfected, your allocated time will be up and early years will be waiting outside the hall, ready for their afternoon parachute session.

For the most part, rehearsals will be a tedious loop of repetition. Telling children, the same thing over and over and making little to no progress on actual scenery or story development. 'Stand here!', 'Sit down!', 'With feeling!' and 'Louder!' will be the main directions barked at everyone and anyone for the first five weeks of your six-week rehearsal schedule. Despite being given their roles of choice, nicely highlighted scripts, allowances for the odd missed rehearsal, and even one-to-one time to 'build confidence', the children will usually take right up until the dress rehearsal to get everything right. Or as right as can be. After weeks of screaming 'Louder!', organising, watching mistake after mistake, and changing scripts, you will eventually reach production week. At this point, your nerves are shot!

Production week:

By the time production week comes around, you will be happy if you never have to watch another version of your chosen production again! Fumbled lines, mispronounced names, shoddy scenery, and both overzealous and underwhelming performances to date will have you on your knees praying for it all to end. In reality, the to-do list will be ever growing. With days to go until your dress rehearsal, it's not uncommon to still have outstanding, complete costumes. Which several parents have promised to make but, to date, have not materialised. As well as a whole cast run through, completed scenery, distributed tickets, flyers and poster, and your lead boy / girl who have been off for the last two days with 'the flu'.

Despite all this, you have a strict deadline and will soon be eating into morning lesson to get everything done. In my experience, Literacy lessons become poster and ticket making sessions, Numeracy lessons become adding up how much times we have to get everything right, and Phonics lessons become ad-hoc singing to the production CD lessons while teaching how to lip-sync and smile at the same time. A last minute, a mad-rush will see your children sticking posters in every conceivable window, advertising showtime dates, times, and ticket prices. Despite best efforts to get your class to make something resembling a professional looking poster, you settle for the last-minute pile of scribbled crap, because you just can't be bothered with detail at this stage. You're desperately ignoring the obvious mistake of 'Tickets only cost £150.00' – as opposed to the £1.50 you wrote on the board.

By the skin of your teeth, you have managed to get tickets made, printed, and at the office ready for all the parents you've never met at parents evening to come see their lovely little angels fluff their lines. Only by working most evenings, making countless calls, and sending numerous emails, parents are now dropping off costumes for all players and the scenery looks like it could pass for finished. At some point, you will have all the costume, a general idea of order, a sense that the children know their scripts, routines and places, and a feeling that this could actually work.

Here you are then, whole school dress rehearsal day. Despite being told this is a run through, a chance to iron out any errors, this is in fact a scrutiny. An opportunity for your head, disgruntled subject leads, teaching assistants, and parent helpers to see what the last six weeks disruption has all been about. You will tell your children exactly as you have been told yourself, that this is a run through and a chance to iron out any last-minute tweaks or changes. Half of the cast will be nervous; the other half won't really care. As for the rest of the watching school, they want Hollywood!

At some point, you will gather the cast in the hall and position them ready for the start. The lights go down and the whole school will fill the hall. One third of them will be curious, one third of them will be glad to be out of afternoon lessons, and the other third will be EYFS and year 1. So more likely to cry, scream, or be scared by some element to the production. Poised backstage, head in hands, the best you can hope for is your narrator starts on the right page, your lead characters know their own lines, and the lighting technician doesn't plunge everyone into darkness at the mid-point.

Every dress rehearsal I have done has either been a mitigated disaster, children saying each other's lines, reading from scripts, and coming on stage in the wrong scene, or it was an absolute joy. There really is no magic spell to make sure it all goes well in front of the whole school. In some cases, I had children in the early years climb on stage upon seeing a sibling. I have witnessed children refuse to go up on stage because everyone is watching. I've even had better dress rehearsals than on the night performances. When it comes to productions, you only ever know when the lights go up.

Despite everyone's best efforts and the echo of, 'Don't worry, this is a run through for you before the big night' ringing in your ears, you will always be subjected to constructive feedback from some busy body member of staff. You know it wasn't perfect. You know they weren't loud enough for the people at the back of the hall. You know that various minor characters fluffed their lines. And of course, you know you only selected the obvious choices for the lead roles. Suddenly everyone is an expert! The lighting wasn't the best, the scenery was a bit amateur, there was messing about backstage and, 'Did that really take six weeks practise?' No end of people will all have their say. All of which were asked to produce the end of year show but declined due to 'other commitments'. What you may find, though, is that one teaching assistant or teacher may just pat you on the back and say, 'Well done'. That there will be the reason you don't tear out all your hair pre-performance night.

Performance night(s):

Most schools, in my experience, will offer parents a choice of two evening shows and an afternoon performance. This way, there is an equal opportunity for everyone to select a time suitable for them to watch their little angels perform, take numerous photographs, and try to bag the seats closest to the front. I've never understood why some parents turn up to every show. I mean, I understand your sense of pride, especially if your child has a lead role, but to watch the same show three times?

In my experience, performance day / night is nerve wracking for all involved. The children spend all day wanting to get ready. You spend all day trying to teach a normal timetable, while desperately wanting to sneak in another quick run through, and the office spends all day taking messages about reserving seats and confirming start times. With over-excited children buzzing off their nut all day and you're just thinking about the negative feedback from the dress rehearsal, it suddenly dawns on you that the big day is here. The costumes are waiting in the hall, the stage needs dressing, as do the children, the seats need putting out, and you're not totally convinced everyone knows their lines. But hey-ho, it showtime.

I learnt over the years, the quicker you can get everyone changed and in position the better. It really is not worth leaving this until thirty minutes before doors-open. You are simply setting yourself up to fail. For a 5 p.m. start I would always recommend a 4 p.m. change time. Sooner than this and there is a risk of buttons being unpicked, stitching coming undone, and costumes getting dirty and bedraggled by the wearer. Attempt the change later and there are equally as many risks. Such as costumes not fitting, last minute alterations, sweaty, and stroppy children, or costumes being misplaced. I always found the hour before gave enough wiggle room for all of the above, as well as a pre-show chat.

The pre-show chat is a vital element of any successful show. To date, the children neither talk nor sing loud enough. There have been a few issues with rotating scenery, thanks to the scenery managers. Who by the way, have only one role: to rotate the scenery boards when the lights go down? Everyone who enters onto the stage stomps like a giant, thus making all tentative scenery shake. Background / crowd extras are always in the wrong place and finally, your sound technician cannot cue up the songs exactly at the right time. The pre-show chat is aimed at reducing stress, both the cast and yours, instilling confidence, and ensuring everyone knows what to say, where to be, and what to do. I always found a calm, pre-dressed, sit-down worked well. The idea was to make sure the children knew I had confidence in them. They wanted to hear, 'You can do this' or 'Everything will be ok, just do your best'. This is what they got, 'I just want you all to know how very proud I am of you getting to this point. Sitting here with you and seeing you all dressed up, I know we will have a good show. I want you all to stand tall, speak loudly, sing proud, and just think how happy your parents will be sat in the audience, watching you. Focus on your lines, you know them anyway. Remember to sing with pride, you all know the words. Finally, remember this is your end of year show, your moment, and your production. So, whatever you do, do it for yourself and your classmates. We have done this 1000 times; we know what we need to do. So, let's go and do it!' It's at this point you, the teacher, realise you have suddenly transformed into a Hollywood director, who actually gives a toss about the whole thing!

It's not a magical formula, but it always worked for me. Children would high five one another and share the sense they could do it. Now all you need is a black t-shirt for the scenery manager, who turned up in fluorescent green thinking this is perfectly acceptable because, 'No-one will see me when the lights are out'.

Come rain or shine, the queues of parents will form outside the hall a good half hour before start time. Meaning only one thing: They have to be let in early and witness last minute preperations. Once seated, the parents and carers think this is the perfect time to seek out their angels and grab a quick photograph. Not on my watch! All children were strictly told beforehand, 'Pictures can be taken during or after the show. We don't want to spoil our costumes or reveal any of the story before we start'.

In the absence of the sound technician, who has just decided it's time for a toilet break, you'll find yourself rushing to the sound system to play the appropriate entrance music to drown out the chattering parents. Once done, the lights will dim, the music will fade, and as the first spotlight comes on, there is little more you can do. Except sit in the front row with a script, pray, make small but obvious hand gestures, and just hope the stage doesn't get plunged into darkness.

When it comes to producing the end of term show, I must admit, it was a role I truly enjoyed. Not because I got to boss round children, dress them in costumes and skip art, music, and history for a term. No, more because the end result was usually some of the best work you would produce that year. After weeks of screaming, crying, shouting, and general exhaustion, the first night production makes it all worthwhile. Children will magically find their voices and speak so that everyone in the hall can hear them. Songs will be sung in tune and with such passion they'd be the envy of any professional choir. Jokes, within the script, will be delivered with perfect timing and audiences will bellow with laughter. Lights dimmed and shone at perfect times. Music played and paused with precision and perfect volume. The icing on the cake? All scenery rotated in perfect unison and with seamless transition. To finish off, the audience all clap with rapturous applause and join in singing the finale song. What more could you ask for?

Despite all your doubts, fears, and positive feedback, they only go on to pull out the best performance you could have hoped for. Thus, making you look like Steven Spielberg and feeling like an absolute Rockstar. I always rewarded my class for a job well done, despite the outcome. This was usually sweets, time off lessons, or extra playtime. Just as an acknowledgement and to make them feel like I really did appreciate them. I had to remember, when all said and done, they were children, not trained actors. In spite of the weeks of stress, that first night and subsequent performances would stay with them for the rest of the year and could easily be the highlight of their time in primary school. When all the performances had been done, the costumes, stage, and scenery packed away, we, as a class, always looked back at where we started and where we ended. If a governor or parent had filmed the performance, we always watched it back. It was an excellent opportunity for the children to see themselves. After all, they never truly saw what they had done otherwise. Reflecting back and laughing at one another was often as much fun as the show itself, and something I truly believe the children enjoyed doing.

I would recommend every teacher try their hand at producing an end of term show. There is little doubt it is stressful, in more ways than it should be. Children will test your patience, as will parents. Staff un-associated with the year group or the production will be of little help unless pushed. You'll face obstacle after obstacle, especially if anything needs paying for. You'll need to be on your A-game with your organising skill, diplomacy, and even be prepared for last minute pushbacks and change. Despite all of this, the end result when it comes off is a magical feeling. Uncooperative children, poor readers, terrible singers, and the worst behaved members of your class all come together for one common goal: To give their parents and carers the best end of year production they can. And they do.

Most parents will praise you and your children's efforts, beaming with pride and full of handshakes, and, 'Well done'. Fellow teachers will pat you on the back, if not for a great show, then for getting them out of afternoons lessons for one day. Your head may well even acknowledge the effort you have made, not as much as they praise the children, though, and congratulate you on such a great show. Nobody will ever know what you put into making it all happen. The time, the effort, the passion, and the determination to just do well, except you. At some point, you will reflect back and see it was all worth it. You'll praise yourself for a job well done and vow, never to do it again. In reality, if you're a year 6 teacher, you'll do it every year, and every year will be the same routine. But the end result will be better than the year before. Now, why can't it ever go that well for SATS revison?!

Teachers Behaving Badly

Just remember, everything you do reflects on the school

As a child, if I ever saw one of my teachers outside of school, for some reason I always avoided them. I'd duck my head, cross the road, turnaround and go back on myself, or just plain ignore them. The teacher on the other hand, would always make some sort of noticeable contact. An over excited wave, a huge, uncomfortable looking smile, or some sort of funny shuffle in my direction. I don't know why I acted this way. I guess the thought of seeing and speaking to a teacher outside of school was just not cool, or the done thing. As I got older, the thought of seeing a teacher in the pub, a night club, or somewhere more normal, such as a car wash, never crossed my mind. At the time I just assumed, albeit rightly or wrongly, that I'd never bump into a teacher in a club as they were just too old they and would never go to the same places as me. Teachers then were just not seen as...well, people with lives, I guess. They were just teachers in their chinos, cardigans, parted hair, and uncool cars. Why would they be out in the pub?

As a trainee teacher, you are presented with the 'teacher standards.' The teacher standards are issued by the department for education (DFE) and set minimum requirements for teachers' practice and conduct. The standards are set by law and every teacher must follow them, unless there is a good reason not to. The standards are used to assess the performance of all teachers and can be applied to your conduct both inside and outside of school. Part two of the teacher standards relates to personal and professional conduct. Within part two the standards state: 'A teacher is expected to demonstrate consistently high standards of personal and professional conduct'. Then follows a list of what is deemed acceptable behaviour and attitudes, which set the required standard for conduct throughout a teacher's career. As a trainee teacher, it is drilled into you the importance of following and upholding these standards.

It always amused me as a trainee teacher, effectively a student, that you were rigorously reminded of these standards, while also being surrounded by two-for-one offers at the student bar, free entry to nightclubs, and alcohol promotions specifically aimed at you...the student! It's like everyone else in university could go nuts but you, the trainee teacher, who had standards to uphold. So, you had to act like a monk. Needless to say, me and my cohort did not. There is no separation between students when it comes to drinking.

As a fully qualified and employed teacher, there is an expectation that you are, or will become, a pillar of the community and a role model. Suddenly, you are seen as having this weight of responsibility that you must carry at all times, and always project the image of a sensible, kind, and caring member of your community. Specifically, if you teach in the same community you live in. You understand that being a teacher means people will see you differently and make certain assumptions about you prior to knowing you. This is hard to adjust to and carries its own weight upon your already very heavy shoulders. You understand that, in the big bad world beyond the school gates, parents and children will still see you as 'Mr' or 'Miss'. Which means showing a certain level of constraint. What you don't understand, or at least I never did, is this idealistic vision that the community holds will extend to and encroach on your personal life, too.

It's only once you are qualified that you begin to realise how the children you teach seem to pop up everywhere. You'll be shopping in your local

182

supermarket and see them, suddenly becoming aware of the contents of your trolley. You'll see them in restaurants and other eateries and start to doubt your decision for fish and chips. (It's not the healthy option you teach about, is it?) You'll also notice just how many pubs are child friendly, usually as you're sipping the first, ice-cold beer on a sunny Saturday afternoon. You suddenly become increasingly aware that the children you teach pop up everywhere and, unlike when I was growing up, children are neither afraid nor embarrassed to see you. In fact, some positively brim with pride at seeing you and want to come say hello. You, being the local pillar of the community, heartily oblige and make the effort to say hello, too. These encounters are magnified should you take the somewhat stupid decision to teach at your local primary school (yes, I did). It seemed like a good idea at the time. Easy to get to, you know the area, and you wanted to be part of the local community. (How wrong I was!) You soon learn to bank a standard response to both parents and children depending on the time and place you encounter them. You learn that smiling and politeness usually pays dividends and, more importantly, you will soon learn where to eat and drink without seeing half of your classroom judge you while you relax. Chance meetings in public places will become common and, to be fair, you will usually get away with a polite hello or a nod and a smile.

In my experience, the time teachers tend to relax the most is when they are surrounded by other teachers. Yes, they are all aware of the standards and yes, they have all perfected the art of following them for most of the school day. In social situations, when teachers get together, the standards get thrown out the window. The best way to get to know your workmates is to go out with them. While this can be said of any workplace, nowhere is it truer than when you work in a school. I have worked in many schools and the need to get out, let it all hang-out, and generally 'go for it' is always apparent. Regardless of where I have worked. Nowhere will you truly see behind the teacher mask than on a social night out surrounded by teachers. English teachers swearing like a sailor. Math teachers so drunk they can't calculate what they owe on the round, and just chuck in a tenner. Headteachers necking Sambuca shots like their life depends on it. And PE teachers, the fittest of the fit, chowing down on kebabs to soak up the thirteen pints they've just nailed. In safe, well-established groups teachers will revert back to their student days and forget the rules, forget the standards and, at times, forget their underwear! It's amazing to be part of it, too. In some schools you may only ever see, communicate, and pass time with staff from other year groups. It could be days, even weeks, before a year 6 teacher communicates with someone from early years. Especially if the school has a key stage one and a separate key stage two building. You don't communicate properly in staff meetings. Ideally, you want to get out of them as soon as possible. In-service days are all about clusters. The year group clusters, the friendship clusters, and the management clusters. At some point you'll be sat in nominated groups, so there's no chance to catch-up properly anyway. Add to this, you never know who is listening and there's little room for real conversations. A good, whole school night out is always well received and usually the best chance to meet your 'real' colleagues.

In an article published by the Telegraph-in 2008, the number of teachers facing discipline for bad behaviour outside of school was on the rise. To add to this, the article listed drink driving, drug taking, and fraud as the most common reasons for teachers getting into trouble, even fired. While I cannot verify the authenticity of the article, I can definitely verify that I have socialised with teachers who have taken class A drugs (a head teacher), driven home after several pints (office staff), had sexual relationships with one another (I lived with a teacher who was 'seeing' a lunchtime supervisor), and who have been into, and caused actual physical punch-ups fights (male and female staff!). To be fair, I have never known a teacher who has committed fraud! I am by no means judging, I too was guilty of several of these misdemeanours

The level of misbehaviour on a teacher's night out has never failed to astound me. Both as an observer and participant (usually the latter!). The most common behaviour trait is casual drug taking. I have known teaching assistants, subject leaders, senior members of staff, and even head teachers all partake in drug use. Ranging from a smoking pot in the pub garden to cocaine use in the pub toilets. While this is not shocking to me (live and let live I say), I have no doubt it would be to parents and governors of the school. Teachers are, after all, humans, so why should they behave any differently than bankers, lawyers, and doctors when on a night out? All of the said professions, I am sure, take part in similar social behaviours. Are we expected to believe that your local G.P or emergency doctor isn't sleeping with at least one of the nurses he or she works with? Do we walk into a bank and worry if the cashier spends their weekends at wild swinging parties? Does anyone care if the local estate agent dresses in a leather gimp suit and snorts coke off his workmate's chest on a Saturday night? I expect not. So why should the rules be different for teachers? Because of the standards!

It is highly likely you have encountered a teacher who has broken some, if not all, of the teacher standards socially. In schools across the country, teachers are having sexual relationships with one another. Teachers are sleeping with dinner ladies, kitchen staff, teaching assistants, and parents (again, I pass no judgement as a guilty party). I have worked with teachers who carried out affairs with parents. I also include myself in this. It happens. There is nothing wrong with this. The important thing is not to let anyone else know that it's happening. As a teacher, where else are you supposed to meet someone? School life is all consuming and your life revolves around it. This may not be the view of a headteacher if a teacher is having a relationship with a parent. While no ethical or professional standard is being broken, there is the issue of moral standards to be considered and how this may affect any teacher / pupil relationship. The practise of inter school relationships is more common than both children and parents probably know. I cannot think of one school I worked in where teacher and parent, teacher and helper, or teacher and teacher were not 'at it' it some form. The key to keeping this between those involved is obvious to those partaking in the relationship: be discreet, seek approval from the head (If it's serious), don't let the children know, and try to refrain from kissing and having sexual contact in the stationary cupboard!

As stated, I am not without sin in behaving badly. During my time teaching there were many opportunities to break the moral code that came with teaching. It all started well. My first teaching role was at a church school, so opportunity for bad behaviour would surely be restricted to the other side of the school gate. Well, not strictly true. I must acknowledge the fact that as an out-and-out atheist, I probably displayed bad behaviour from the moment I walked in the door. I worked on the basis that, if there is a God, I would be struck down for the charlatan I was and be revealed in front of everyone. As this did not happen, I let you draw your own conclusion (I can honestly state, no relationships took place at this stage of my teaching journey). My first experiences of teaching life began on a moral lie. I had no belief in the higher power but had to display, at interview and beyond, that I had no issues delivering 'The word of the Lord' to the children... Whatever pays the bills! To add to this, there was also the issue of the sign of the cross. I had paid no consideration to the process, and it was week three before a child, aged eight, told me I was doing it wrong. In all senses of the phrase, 'Bless him', he got me out of a spot there. So, there I was, an N.Q,T in a faith school, with little to no faith, and a distinct lack of awareness of any higher being. In this case it was believed that was God. For many reasons, I soon began to realise this was not the school for me. Despite my horrendous experiences of an ECT mentor, which I have reflected on previously, it was soon apparent that my specific personality was not aligned to this school (loud mouthed and unfiltered). I struggled to gel with anyone. My sense of humour and humoristic approach to unknown situations soon began to rise above my actual ability as a teacher. I left, mid-point in my N.Q,T year and found a more suitable school.

My new school was less me, than me, but more me than my previous school. A small village school in an affluent area, populated with well to do children, parents, and helpers. It was here, as one of only two male members of staff, I began to see how easy it was to involve parents in 'extracurricular activities.' My partner teacher was at a crisis point. His marriage was in tatters as his affair with a teaching assistant had been revealed. Everyone in the village knew about it and, rather than make them cautious of the new male member of staff, mums, aunts, and grandmas seemed to flock to my class in abundance. I held a 'meet the teacher' evening where more females turned up than males. Notably made up, dressed very well, and with a distinct lack of buttons on their shirts, blouses, and dresses. Yes, this was the school for me after all! Nights out here were few and far between, the school was tiny, and the majority of staff were aging. The nights out were... cosy and full of innuendos. My first real taste of this side of school life. While I maintained a professional relationship with all staff and parents, I did have nights out with a few 'yummy mummies', as well as a very serious relationship with a divorcee parent who had children in my class. As this relationship developed, I moved to another school after two years. My new school was bigger, more diverse (There were three males in this school!) and by this time, my situation had changed, and I was a married man.

What I quickly learnt at this school was the larger the staff count, the more likely the opportunity to behave badly. Within a term, I had the opportunity to be drawn into 'the dark side' where infidelity was the norm, and casual drug misuse was rife. I adapted quickly. While firmly managing to keep my fidelity in check, despite advances from cleaners and kitchen staff. Moving through schools, local authorities and year groups, the model stayed the same, but wore many faces. Male teachers seemed to be subjected to as much sexual harassment as anyone. But it was less obvious and, perhaps more welcome. In every school, there were undertones of sexual tension between male and female staff. Rumours were rife about in school affairs, sexual misconduct, and private classroom shenanigans. While I remain no angel, I did carry on a school relationship under the very noses of my colleagues for quite some time (by this time my marriage had long since dissolved). In the end, I confessed to my head, and we were 'outed' during a night out. I don't think anyone really cared. As I said, it's obvious if you're single, you will more than likely meet your partner at school.

While I do not advocate any behaviours that could ultimately cost anyone their job, it is inevitable that standards will be broken. Especially outside of school. Teachers do get horrifically drunk, get into arguments that may lead to fights, and if so inclined, seek alternative ways to relax and to party. This may include drugs. The expectation that teachers will somehow be above and beyond certain social etiquettes is unrealistic. The job has many stresses and unrealistic expectations itself. Being a teacher is a hard, stressful, and demanding role, unknown to those who don't do it or have never known a teacher themselves. Have teachers ever gone to work with a hangover? Of course, they have, it's a rite of passage as an ECT. Has a teacher ever arrived at work drunk, or driven to work drunk? Not to my knowledge, but that doesn't make it an automatic no. Have teachers ever turned up to work stoned? Again, not in my experience, yet it doesn't mean they haven't. Teachers are like every other stressful profession; they will always seek ways to relax and enjoy themselves.

While each one of them remain aware of the teacher standards, should these matter on Saturday night at 3 a.m.? That's a matter of opinion. As long as your child's teacher does not risk the safety or well-being of your child, or their class, should you care what they do beyond the school gates? Is it in the public's interest to know which teachers are having sex with which lunchtime supervisors or parents? The gossips of the playground mafia will always concoct stories. The worst and most harsh critics of the teacher are the parents. You can be criticised for wearing the wrong jacket, having the wrong hair style, or even driving a car which is above and beyond theirs. They will always find something to gossip about and if it's not you, it will be your partner teacher or another colleague. Nothing you do will stop the playground mafia from gossiping. All you have to do is make sure you pick your confidants carefully, ensure nothing is confirmed with any parent, and

don't get caught taking your hip flask to swimming
lessons!

Inset Days

Just another day-off for teachers

During my time as a child in school, any excuse for a day off was a good day. Snow day, boiler failure, or flood. If they equated to a day-off, we were ecstatic. As a kid, to be given the day off unexpectedly was like Manna from heaven. While I'm sure my own parents scrambled around, rearranging their days and organising who was going to do what; during this unscheduled day off, I don't ever recall my parents calling up the school or confronting school staff to complain at the inconvenience of it all. I'm certain, though my mind is foggy on the frequency when it happened, we just got on with it and coped. I don't remember work being sent home, topics having to be done, or recount work detailing how I spent the day being requested. No, I'm pretty sure that on snow days, we went out and played in the snow. And on other days, grabbed our bikes and went off cycling into the woods. While I'm not recalling in great detail here, what I did some thirty-five plus years ago as a child, my point is I don't remember unscheduled days off school being frequent or problematic.

Inset (**IN-SE**rvice **T**raining) days were introduced in the late 1980²s by the conservative government and were initially known as 'Baker days'. This was, I believe, about the same time the national curriculum was introduced. It makes sense then that my primary school years were left uninterrupted by any unscheduled days off as I left primary school in the mid-eighties. While it must have been that my secondary school days were affected by inset days, I don't recall too much time being off school as a result. Although by this time I was adept at bunking-off and dodging days when the mood took me.

An inset day, also known as TD days (Teacher development), PD days (Professional development), and a CPD days (Continuing professional development) is one of a series of scheduled days in most schools in the United Kingdom. These days are teaching where pupils do not need to attend school, but the staff are requested to attend some form of training. The content could be related to the implementation of new technology, new government initiatives, new school policies, or new ways of doing things within the school which cannot be implemented with children present. These days are vital for teachers to make the time to become familiar with any changes within government or changes implemented by the local authority. Especially if you are new to a school. In addition, it may be that the school needs to review and amend its marking, behaviour, or assessment policy and all staff are required to know the how's and whys before it is implemented. In other jobs, training is part of your normal working day. In teaching your normal working day involves many, many pupils. All with differing needs and abilities. On the job training happens all the time, but scheduled training cannot happen when children are present. A hard fact to understand for the non-teaching community.

It is common practise, as well as good practise, that schools plan these days and inform parents at the start of the academic year. It is normal for a school to have five inset days a year, which will be allocated by the local authority. It is not unusual for these inset days to be tagged onto the start or the end of a term. Two inset days at the start of a new September term (Term 1) is not uncommon, nor is an inset day at the end of the summer term (July).

It seems that parents are mostly baffled, and sometimes angry, that schools take inset days. The attitude, 'Oh it's yet another day off for teachers' is quite common. To those parents who don't know a

196

teacher (And let's be honest, all of them do!) or have spent time talking to a teacher about workload, inset days are an inconvenience. It's another day they have to spend with their own child or make arrangements for said child to be off-loaded with another adult. In some of the more deprived areas I have taught in, the inconvenience is about disrupting a scheduled nail appointment or mid-afternoon meeting in the pub. Parents don't always know, care, or even understand why inset days happen. I can totally understand why, in some cases, it does frustrate parents when these days are scheduled. And they are not given the details of what will happen during that day. The most common complaint I got regarding inset days was that parents didn't even know what we were doing that warranted 'another day off'. In my experience, schools communicate all sorts of things with parents: dinner money arrangements, uniform requirements, school trips, even recycling targets and goals. But very rarely – if ever – were parents told what skills the teachers would learn on a scheduled inset day. It seems a really small amount of effort to make to pacify and inform parents. All they need to know is whether the day is focussed on Numeracy, Literacy, or policy amendment. It seemed to me, if parents knew in advance it would at least arm them with information before they got the hump and accused teachers of 'just another day off'.

Inset days were always much less exciting than parents ever imagined. A far cry away from the lazy days of 'slacking off' that they imagined. To me, I would rather have been in my class with thirty children, than attending any inset day.

The first inset days of the year at the start of term one was equally the best and worst they would ever be. The nicer elements of it are there were always more opportunities to grab a hot coffee, and there were more biscuits than usual. But really, they were never very enjoyable (The day, not the biscuits). Day one, everyone is usually bright, breezy, and looking forward to seeing one another. I was never one of those teachers who stayed in touch over the summer holidays. Yes, I would send the odd text or email to discuss planning and routine. But beyond week one of the summer, I didn't want to hear from any teacher in my school until I went back in September. This was not the case for everyone. In some schools there is always that incestuous circle of friends who can't possibly go the whole six weeks without seeing one another. As such they arrange play-dates for their children, or coffee so 'We don't lose contact'. Ugh! It made me scream inside seeing two, three, or four colleagues who couldn't stand to be apart and needed to check-in with one another, for fear of missing out on some vital summer term gossip!

In my mind, the summer term was mine and I'd meet everyone on first day back. Inset day one always has a nice atmosphere about it. You meet back up with familiar faces, share some stories with your close colleagues, and recount the freedom of the summer holidays. It's an opportunity to chat over coffee, eat some homemade cake, usually baked by a teaching assistant (On some occasions even I made cake for the inset days), and generally make yourself feel less terrible about the upcoming day, week, and term. Slowly, but surely, you'd relax into your place and feel nicer about returning to work surrounded by, some, friends and colleagues. One of the few days you can go to school in jeans, a thick jumper, and even a hat if you had not bothered to arrange your hair that morning.

The first day of term, inset day one, is also monotonous and full of dread. The stark reality of back to work soon kicks in as the clock strikes 9 a.m. Once you have poured your coffee, caught up with friends and just about dunked your first biscuit, the school bell rings and... bang! Everyone shuffles into their seat, sat in their little groups. The head teacher, or resentful deputy, will walk around and hand out an agenda of events starting at 9.00 a.m. and (If you're lucky) finishing at 4.00 p.m. As you look at it, you seek out break times and lunchtime, mentally planning your day around breaks and food. As you glare at the agenda, you look at bold titles prescribing your day and all the letters jumbling into one as you realise this is going to be a long day.

Inevitably there will be the false 'welcome back' speech by the head, as well as the 'glad to see you all back looking so fresh' nonsense and then the order of the day. In the event you may have forgotten how to read over the summer, a large agenda is projected onto the screen before you and each event read out in turn. The lists are endless: Review of marking policy, assessment of last year's results, behaviour modification techniques, safeguarding... It's not even 9:15 a.m. and you're already thinking about the 10:30 a.m. coffee-break. As your day is dictated to you, you begin to realise that most of the morning has been set aside to review policies, which were reviewed in the last staff meeting. So why on Earth are we revisiting them now? Worse than this, you note that, at 11:00 a.m. just after coffee, you see the heading 'SEN improvements with Barbara Bingley'. Who is Barbara Bingley and what is she going to improve about SEN (Special Educational Needs)? Before the first activity, you are shuffled over to mixed key-stage groups. Because, 'It's better to increase awareness of who does what in their year groups'. Veiled speak for, 'I know if I keep that group together, they will draw faces and rude words on the handouts', and 'There is no way those two can stay there given what happened on the end of term night out!' You reluctantly move to your designated table and realise, out of a group of six, you've never actually spoke to three of these people and don't recognise two others. What on Earth is going on?

As the morning unfolds, you begin to feel only slightly less awkward sitting in your group, and you paw your way through page upon page of PowerPoint handouts. Occasionally there's a group question, or discussion point, where you add a 'Yeah, me, too' or even a, 'Well, what do the group think?' type comment, so you can justify your own reasons for getting out of bed.

Eventually, you are dismissed for the much-needed coffee break. As you gather to the staffroom and try to grab a cake or sugary snack, you lock eyes with your end-of year encounter. A moment's awkwardness, then you move on. Shuffling through the crowds, you realise someone is drinking from your mug. Your dedicated, brought from home, end of year present that someone else is sipping from. No panic, there's always the chipped, tea-stained mug at the back of the cupboard. Coffee poured, the milk is gone, excellent! Before you even begin to think, the bell sounds, and you're ordered back to your table. Chipped mug filled with black coffee; off you return for more dribble. As you sit, you see a face unfamiliar to you and your table. You whisper and makes assumptions until finally someone looks at the agenda. Ah, the elusive and unknown Barbara Bingley. The section on SEN, oh what joy!

The one thing I always hated about inset days, staff meetings and the like was having to listen to people / guest speakers who would come in, talk to you, preach to you, and generally talk down to you about your teaching methods, having never taught themselves. The 'experts' on behaviour management. The 'leaders' in positive reinforcement. The 'advisors' on time management. All well and good and I'm sure very good at their roles, but who are they to come in and tell us / me how to teach, having never set a foot into a teacher's shoe in their whole lives? These, in my view, were the worst kind of people to be forced to listen to. 'Experts' in education and how it works. People, paid by the local authority or the school, coming in to talk to me about how to improve my chances of positive behaviour in my class. Standing there, showing me glossy images from an ideal school where every child smiles, and behaviour is not an issue. Talking their way around how to not argue with a child, or how to restrain a child without actually touching them or invading their own space. What a load of old crap! These people, having never taught, never had a child spit at them, or been sworn at by a child, standing there telling me how to 'react with calm and peace in all circumstances' made my blood boil. As did their Maslow hierarchy of needs pyramids!

To make things worse, today's speaker, Barbara, was here to tell us how we can improve our SEN provisions. Despite their best efforts, these people rarely kept me engaged or interested in anyway. Unless they came armed with sugary snacks, sweets, or cakes it was back to the doodling of stick men and boobs, onto my agenda. Despite having many occasions where guest speakers came to inset days, I learned (or tried to learn) a valuable lesson: Always pay attention, because they will ask questions and they will have noticed you doodling and generally zoning out. Never did this once resonate, but always did I fall foul to it. One thing I could guarantee is that I'd always be asked a question by the speaker. Always! The point in the day where I wanted the ground to open up and swallow me. Now if you worked with me, you would never have been surprised that I could never give an answer when in this situation. Or reverted to some comical, jovial response trying to cover my arse. If, however, this was your first day at school, maybe you were an ECT or a new teaching assistant, I would have looked like the incompetent arse I was no doubt portraying myself to be. I once recall I was asked to give my input on something I had not paid attention to so, to deflect, I asked the speaker, 'What school is it you said you taught at?' As the eyes of the head, deputy, and other senior leaders pierced my soul, I sank into my chair, awaiting my call to the office at the next break.

In some cases, inset day lunches can be the best lunch you will eat. Possibly the only lunch you will eat all year. Some schools will call in the kitchen team and they will cook the meal for you. Inevitably the same grey, meat free fish fingers you encountered on your interview day with soggy chips and beans. No need to be glum though, as it's inset day, you can have six fish fingers! On the other hand, some schools will get external caterers to provide lunch, and these schools are the ones where lunchtimes are a joy. You go back to the staff room and find a plethora of silver plates with a variety of sandwiches, crisps, savoury snacks, and cake. Truly the best part of any inset day. There will always be one member of staff who complains about the lack of variety, the lack of vegan options, or wrong flavour crisps. To these members of staff, I would always ask, 'Did you bring your own lunch?'

while resisting the urge to tell them to, 'Shut the hell up'. These lunches were always worth savouring. Some staff would go to their classrooms and tend to display or cover some books. Not me. I sat and enjoyed every snack and every treat I could, knowing that the afternoon session would no way be as engaging as the morning session. Sure enough, glancing at the agenda, the afternoon is filled with 'response to marking', 'the new planning proforma', and 'daily recap'.

An inset afternoon is so much harder than a class teaching afternoon. During that time, you return back from lunch full of food, treats. and cake. Or heavy with council grey fishfingers and holding a coffee as you stagger back to your seat. The agenda dictates that the next hour will be spent completing a book scrutiny and sharing ideas with your key stage partner on how you can improve the levels in writing moving forward. After this you have a dedicated hour for 'classroom time'. An hour to sort your classroom, making any changes to the environment, prior to the little angels coming back in; just short of one day away.

The reality is, you'll struggle to be of any value to anyone during the 'scrutiny' because you're full-up, tired and bored of the whole monotony of the day so far. Your interest probably left the building at midmorning, and the excitement of the afternoon doesn't look like it'll be keeping you awake. In stark contrast to this, an afternoon teaching is far more exciting. You could be spending this time teaching P.E, Science, art, history, or French. Surrounded by a class full of excitable children bursting at the seams to learn, entertain, and even annoy you. For now, you have three more hours to go and all you can think about is the drive home. Inset afternoons drag. They appear to freeze time and no amount of toilet breaks, coffee refills, or left-over jelly babies make time go quicker. You are so far away from the 'jolly' that the parents think you are having, it seems you may as well get stuck in and crack on with the task in hand.

There is always a quiet calmness to the afternoon sessions. Not concentration, just pure boredom and the inevitable come down of the sugar filled morning. Eventually, home time will be within reach, but not before the handout questionnaire on how the day went. Each person is handed one and, despite the promise of anonymity, you know that your head knows your handwriting style. So be careful how you respond. How was the day? What did you find most useful and why? What will you take-away from today to implement in the year? What do you think could be done better and why? I'm unsure if anyone ever answers these honestly, but as with the whole day, they are a tick box exercise which must be completed. As you leave, you have the pleasure of knowing tomorrow you can do it all again! Never will there be a time when you pray for children to be in school than when you start or finish an inset day.

In my experience, inset days come joined to holiday time or long weekend;. Prompting the false belief from parents that these days are extra time off those teachers want to shorten the term. Worse still, where parents are not informed as to the purpose of the inset, they become convinced these days are pointless and just an inconvenience. While this is far from true, it must be agreed that children deserve teachers whose development and growth are supported by school and local authorities. If this is to be the case, then inset days need to be seen as the valuable experiences they can and should be.

It would make sense that all schools should have a moral duty to inform parents, not only when inset days are, but what they are about, too. Surely, if parents know what inset days will comprise of and why the time is essential for teachers, then the anger, annoyance, and misunderstanding will become less. And parents will be grateful that their teachers are taking time to invest in their own development, and therefore their own children's futures. When it comes to CPD, parents are dealing with information black holes, they are blocked out. If schools and teachers want parents to get behind and support teacher CPD, then they need to inform parents and pull away any veil of mystery surrounding CPD and inset days.

As for you, the teacher, unfortunately these days form part of your teacher's pay and conditions document (In maintained schools). So, you are obliged to attend. The best you can hope for is engaging, motivating days, with inspired sessions, dedicated targets for you and your children, a great lunch and a willing bunch of staff. All dedicated to making the days purposeful and justified. At worse… Well, you'll be sat in a child's chair, eating soggy chips with grey fishfingers, sat next to and making small talk with Barbara Bingley!

School Holidays

All teachers do is have long holidays

As a young child, school holidays were the best part about school. It seemed like a lifetime before they came, but when they did, how we used to enjoy them. It was never considered, by me at least, what my teacher did during their holiday. I just naturally assumed they went off on extravagant holidays or sat in the library in their cardigans and shoes and just read books. They were teachers and knew everything, right? I had little to no care for my teacher during the holidays, I was too busy riding my bike, climbing and falling out of trees, playing kerby, and running around the neighbourhood with my brother to even care. School holidays were my time to be free from school, free from rules, and they were always too short.

To the outside world, non-teachers and children, your average teacher starts work at eight in the morning and finishes at four in the afternoon.

They have way too many holidays and spend all of them jetting off to destinations far and wide. Spending their over inflated wages on treats parents can't afford. Let's not forget the starting salary for an ECT is £24 ,373, equating to £10.98 per hour and an average primary school teachers pay is £34,500.

Teachers get roughly thirteen weeks holiday a year. Your average primary school teacher works 59.3 hours per week. The reason for these hours is that a lot of time is spent outside of the classroom planning lessons, looking for resources, marking, and other administration tasks. This is so far away from the perceived 8 a.m. – 4 p.m. that many imagine. It is often thought that to be a primary school teacher all you need to do is play with sand and water and know your alphabet. The reality is you will teach on average thirteen lessons a week. All of which need to be: relevant, engaging, interesting, differentiated, and purposeful. In order to do all of this, teachers will spend time outside of the 'normal school day' and find themselves working, in their classes 7:30 a.m. – 5:30 p.m. and beyond.

Another criticism heard by teachers are the objections of parents, children, and other non-teaching staff to in-set / in service days. Often taken in term time and seen as a disruption to the term. Parents will complain that these days are just an excuse for teachers to go into school, extend their holidays, and eat biscuits while they all catch-up with one another. The reality is teachers do require on the job training. New policies and procedures are always coming up, assessment systems changing, and behaviour management systems being changed, Inset days provide schools the opportunity for teachers to become aware of these changes, and agree upon dates when the new changes will be implemented.

When training to become a teacher, it's easy to be attracted to the lure of holidays. Where else offers thirteen weeks paid holidays? The sound of extended Easter and Christmas holidays, with a six-week summer break is appealing, right? What isn't published in the role of class teacher is the very fact that to stay on top of your day-to-day chores, you will spend most of these holidays working. You may work in school or at home, but you will be working for a large proportion of this 'holiday' time.

Teachers do not enjoy the luxury of thirteen weeks down time. No matter which school, which year group, or which subject you lead, there will never be enough time in the 7:30 a.m. – 5:30 p.m. day to keep on top of all of the jobs you are required to do. This is where holidays come in. The start of any holiday is seen as one of two things: An opportunity to close the books, throw down the marking pen, and start some much-needed time off. It can also be the perfect opportunity to come back into an empty school, empty class, and start ripping down old displays to be replaced by new, up to date, topic specific, shiny displays. Most teachers will take the second option. I understand that teachers need to work additional hours to enable effective changes which help them carry out their professional duties. It seems to be the balance is tipping always in the favour of the school and never in the favour of the teacher.

What is not seen by parents or trainee teachers is that every extra hour or extra day worked by the teacher, is an hour and a day which is unpaid. It comes at zero cost to the teacher and zero cost to the school. By working extra hours, teachers are showing these hours are expendable and not valued, so becomes the new normal. This then devalues the profession and spreads the salary even thinner than it already is.

Do schools expect teachers to work on their own time? Depends on who is asking the question. No head teacher can insist you come in early, stay late, or give up time in your holidays. Not forgetting teachers need to work such hours that enable them to carry out their duties effectively. You will be left to decide when those hours are. I have yet to hear of a teacher who has honestly said, 'I only work during school time, and get all of my tasks completed' and truly meant it. I understand the need to go in during the holidays, all teachers will find a reason to. Be it an administration task, marking, planning, display changing, or general classroom tidy up, all teachers will find a reason. Every teacher will tell themselves, 'I'll just go in for a few hours'. During the half term week, these hours accumulate to days and before you know it, your week off has become two days. Again, this is not seen by parents or children.

While some teachers are resolute in saying, 'My professionalism dictates I work the holidays', does this make them a better teacher? Sure, their displays will be sharper, their rooms may be tidier, and their books may be all up to date. But are they better for it after the holidays? Or just more exhausted than they were pre-holidays? It's hard to find the right balance. While trying to remain a teacher at the top of your game, you will become exhausted. On the other hand, you could be the teacher that works 7:30 a.m. – 5:30 p.m. and enjoys each of your well-earned holidays. But are you worried about what you'll go back to, or how you're perceived? There will never be a fair and manageable balance. As the demands of the job increase, so will the time teachers spend in schools.

The reality is that a teaching year equates to 1,265 dedicated hours, spread across 195 days. Roughly, this works out at £180 per day. As long as teachers feel the need to use their holiday time to stay on top of things, this time may as well be 225 days a year. Spread the salary across the additional thirty days, and is it worth the pay? Or is it just becoming the new normal that teachers will dedicate free, unpaid time for a vocation or a passion? Not forgetting when you do feel comfortable enough and secure enough to book a holiday, you'll pay over the odd prices, be surrounded by parents and children, and very likely cross paths with a current or ex-student who will remind you how lucky you are to get all that time off!

I think it will always be perceived that teaching staff take too many holidays. It will always be the case holidays are cut-short by the need to 'pop into school for one or two jobs.' Parents are quick enough to remind teachers of 'all their holiday', should the need ever arise. What they don't see is the early mornings, late nights, lack of lunch breaks and ever-increasing demands. Given this, if you are a parent, look into your teachers tired, bloodshot eyes and ask yourself 'do they really get paid too much and have too many holidays?'

Your Classroom / School Displays

Your class must be up to date, relevant, and vibrant

As I try to recall my classrooms at school, I don't remember much beyond the seating plan and blackboards. My memory recalls all desks in rows, with the odd desk singled out for the slow learner or misbehaved child. And a huge blackboard that rolled down like a rolodex. I do recall wall displays, but not with any vivid detail. I remember in my English class, a frame at the side of the board and every week the teacher would put a new piece of writing in there. I remember my absolute joy whenever my work appeared on the wall. Other than this writing frame, I'm finding it hard to recall meaningful or purposeful displays in the classroom. I only recall grey, cracked walls and posters reminding us of the Lord's prayer and school rules. The usual, don't run, don't fight etc.

Another way of demonstrating what is going on in both your school and class is the display board.

Schools now have policies on how to create a good display, and teachers are judged over the standard of their class display boards. Some schools have working displays that grow as the learning progresses, and others have informative displays. These show either what has been learnt to date, or what will be learnt. Each school has their own requirements for displays. Some even have dedicated members of staff who plan, organise, and create displays. Some schools insist on double backed walls, double backed edging, learning frames where work is displayed, specific size laminated letters, and a certain percentage of written work to drawn work. The lists can be exhausting just to look at.

So why are displays so important to schools? Maintaining a good display, in terms of the work and the visual element, means schools can display powerful messages about what is valued by them, build a culture of learning through display, and show children that their work is valued. To add to this, there is a view that a powerful display will make a classroom more inviting and encourage learning. As well as them being used to reference learning and become aide memoire for children. In many school's wall displays now form part of a lesson observation, or even form part of a learning walk. A learning walk is the practise where the head, SLT members, or subject leaders walk around the school and observe displays. They make sure appropriate work is displayed, that edges aren't raggedy, staples and pins are inserted neatly, and the work displayed convey an appropriate message. Time well spent, eh? To add to this, not only do displays provide evidence of pupils spiritual, social, and cultural development, but they also can form part of an Ofsted inspection. Hence the need for some schools to place such emphasis on them.

The quality of displays really do vary from school to school and teacher to teacher. The truth behind the matter is, the displays are only as good as the teacher doing them and nobody gets specific training or guidance in how to create a 'good' display. In any school, a display is usually only as good as the classroom next to it, or the one in the corridor. Some teachers can be obsessive about their displays, making sure they are updated daily. Other teachers will put one up, and never change it or reference it again. It really does come down to the teacher and how much time they have to dedicate to a number of displays in their class. Where time is concerned then the usual normal is to whack it up and never reference it again.

I find it astounding there are books out there dedicated to school displays. Whole books giving hints and tips on how to create the 'perfect' display.

Even beyond books, there are websites where you can download display resources and drool at other teachers displays! I mean, this just strikes me as odd. If you are the creative type and have a whole cupboard of display colours and boarders, why do you need to look online or in a book for ideas? Even the least creative person can create something, surely? I mean, books and websites are great, but those authors don't know your class, your children, or your school. So how will replicating their ideas help you? I do accept that some subjects and topics are hard to try and create an interesting display for. In these cases, be the fire starter and allow the children to create the display. Not only can you claim to be a child centric visionary, but you can also blame the whole mess on the children if your head doesn't like it!

To add insult to injury, more often than not, teachers will also be allocated, or asked to nominate, a shared corridor display board. So, as well as the displays in your own classroom, of which you will either have many or not enough, you are now being asked to create a display in a shared space. The problem here lies in that this is a corridor, so everyone from children to visitors will be able to see your creation. Here is where your colleagues either demonstrate their display prowess by creating an all singing, all dancing, illuminated display. Or they whack up a shoddy mess with a mis-spelt heading, unmarked work, and coffee-stained art. Shared space displays add so much stress. People who would not normally visit your class will see them, children and adults alike. A work of art spells disaster as you risk becoming next terms 'Display Coordinator'. And a shockingly bad display with little effort or care, and you risk your entire classroom being held to scrutiny by the whole staff. Who then unleash hell on you in the form of areas to improve?

I hated doing displays. Time consuming, ever developing and always needing to prove that learning was engaging and relevant. For what and for who? Children never gave a damn about them, rarely commented on them, never paid attention to them, even tearing them in their rush to get out of the class. I saw them as brightly coloured reminders of yet another job to complete every term.

Displays are just another thing in a long line of endless jobs on a teacher's list. Some will spend hours lining up letters, trimming backing paper, and forever laminating pieces of art, specially chosen from the best of the best. These teachers will also rotate work daily, making sure each piece of work is marked, contains pupil feedback, is trimmed and double backed. Others will get their teaching assistant to cut both colour backing sheets, straight and frilly edged boarders, and laminate the last piece of work from a top, middle, and bottom child and get them to mount it on the dedicated wall. From that day on, the display won't be added to or touched until later that term when the topic ends and the whole cycle starts again.

About the Author

Growing up, and as far back as I can remember, I never really enjoyed school, until much later. Possibly too late. My early years in playschool were enjoyable. I have vague memories of what I actually did there, other than play with coloured plasticine, eat cheese biscuits, and queue up for small bottles of milk. I do recall making a star shaped Christmas tree decoration from blue card, decorating it with glitter, and having some attempt at my name being written on it. I also believe to this day, my mum still has that piece of art. My journey through school can be summarised as: Infant school, where I was a clumsy child and always falling off things, usually resulting in stiches to my head. Junior school, where (Much to the annoyance of my teachers) I found my voice, my ability to make people laugh, and my passion for writing, acting, and playing the fool (Still not a curriculum subject!). Secondary school, I resisted the urge to learn and fought back against those who made me. I discovered, way too late, if I ever wanted to have a worthwhile job, it all started with education. Finally accepting this, I made my final years in school way too hard for myself and underachieved in abundance.

With a love of anything motorised, petroleum powered and fast, it seems illogical I would train to become a primary school teacher in my late twenties, but this is what I did. I gave up a full-time job in finance, rearranged my outgoings, took the leap, and enrolled in a three-year teaching degree.

Being a teacher was the best job I ever had. It was hard work. It was rewarding. It was the most tiresome role. Everything had to be spot-on, all the time and every day. If you didn't bring your A-game, there was no room for manoeuvre. For a very long time, I loved being a teacher. There was no better feeling than helping inquisitive minds, sharing knowledge, and exploring the world through the eyes of a child. Watching children learn, grow, and develop over a year is a hugely rewarding experience and not something you see in other jobs. Sadly, over time, the job became less about actual teaching and more about bureaucratic red tape, paperwork, and justification. Not what I wanted to become. I didn't leave with a hate for the profession, or a loathing of any teacher. I left for my own sanity.

Forever a life-long lover of dogs, cars, music, and cycling, I continue to work hard, enjoy my free time, and my new found love of writing.

Printed in Great Britain
by Amazon

79667683R00133